BIBLICAL ANSWERS
TO
CATHOLIC QUESTIONS

BIBLICAL
ANSWERS
TO
CATHOLIC
QUESTIONS

GOSPEL
ADVOCATE
A TRUSTED NAME SINCE 1855

OTHER BOOKS BY JOANNE HOWE

A Change of Habit
From Nun to Priest

Published by Gospel Advocate Co.
1006 Elm Hill Pike, Nashville, TN 37210
www.gospeladvocate.com

ISBN 10: 0-89225-592-7
ISBN 13: 978-0-89225-592-4

DEDICATION

This book is affectionately dedicated to Dr. Paul Coffman. Without his biblical knowledge, immeasurable amount of patience, and love for lost souls, I would never have known of God's love, mercy and grace. Because of this, I willingly responded to Christ's invitation to become "born again."

ACKNOWLEDGMENTS

I wish to acknowledge the following individuals who proofread this manuscript and encouraged me to its completion: Jerrie Barber, Marion Barnette, Dr. Rodney Cloud, Jim Olive and Bill Tyner. I am especially grateful to Carolyn Braden for her expertise in the initial proofreading of this manuscript. I would be remiss in not mentioning the following individuals who have been a tremendous support in encouraging me as I wrote this book: Neil Anderson; Debbie Bumbalough; Dr. Dennis Loyd; Jim and Norma Bundy; Bobbye Bryson; Bernice Newell; Mike Lacey; Pat Polston; Valinda Young; Joan Pendergrass; Julia Crawford; my dear sister, Rose Roman; and Dr. Andre Churchwell. I am especially indebted to Debbie McDuffy for her inspiration in addressing this subject and the opportunity she gave me to share this information with her Baptist congregation. God's divine grace has provided the contents of this book using the Holy Spirit's revealed and inspired Word. Without His guidance and teachings, this book may never have come to fruition. To God alone belongs all the glory.

ABOUT THE AUTHOR

Joanne Howe is a native of Pittsburgh, Pa. The oldest of 11 children, she was born Oct. 11, 1935, and was raised as a Roman Catholic. She attended Catholic elementary and high schools. She received her bachelor of arts degree in elementary education with a minor in music from Carlow University in Pittsburgh and her master's degree in counseling from Bowie State University in Bowie, Md. She was one of six finalists for "Teacher of the Year" in 1985 for the state of Maryland.

Howe entered the Sisters of St. Joseph in Baden, Pa., in 1949 and remained in the order for 19 years. She left the convent in 1968 and moved to Laurel, Md. where she spent 29 years as a sixth grade public school teacher. In 1971, she left the Roman Catholic Church to obey the gospel and was baptized for the remission of her sins by Dr. Paul Coffman at the University Park Church of Christ in Maryland.

Howe has written two books, *A Change of Habit* and *From Nun to Priest*, which were published by the Gospel Advocate. *Biblical Answers to Catholic Questions* is her third book. She has also written numerous pamphlets and made videos and a DVD telling of her conversion. She has appeared on several TV programs, radio broadcasts and World Christian Broadcasting recounting her life's story. She has also written several articles for *Christian Woman* and was a former columnist for the *Laurel* (Md.) *Leader*. She was active in community organizations and worked on Capitol Hill in Washington, D.C., for the Republican party.

Lectureships, ladies Bible classes, retreats and inspiration days throughout the United States, Canada, Poland, Czechoslovakia, Yugoslavia, Austria, South Africa and the Far East have included Howe on their programs. Her lessons relate to women in the Bible and the portrait for Christian women in the 21st century.

Howe resides in Hendersonville, Tenn., and attends the Nashville Road Church of Christ in Gallatin, Tenn.

TABLE OF CONTENTS

SECTION 1: BACK TO THE BASICS

QUESTION #1:   How does God define Himself?

QUESTION #2:   How does God explain His existence?

QUESTION #3:   Can we know that God exists today?

QUESTION #4:   Who has given mankind the ability to know the truth about God?

QUESTION #5:   What proofs do we have that there is only one God?

QUESTION #6:   What are the characteristics of God as they are identified in the Bible?

QUESTION #7:   In what form does God exist?

QUESTION #8:   How does each person of the Godhead function?

QUESTION #1:   Who is Jesus Christ?

QUESTION #2:   Why should we believe in Jesus Christ?

QUESTION #3:   What part did Jesus Christ play in man's salvation?

QUESTION #1:   Who is the Holy Spirit?

QUESTION #2:   What are the different names for God's Holy Spirit?

QUESTION #3:   How does God's Holy Spirit function?

QUESTION #4:   When did Christ promise the arrival of God's Holy Spirit, and to whom did He give this promise?

Section 2: Tradition and Truth

A: The Seven Rites (Sacraments) of the Roman Catholic Church

FOREWORD

Solomon said, "Of making many books there is no end, and much study is wearisome to the flesh" (Ecclesiastes 12:12). Estimates indicate that if a person read nothing more than the titles of the books that have been published, it would take him 300 years to read them all (*Ripley's Believe It or Not Catalogue* 1985). However, not all books are the same. Some stand out as having made a difference, not as "wearisome to the flesh" but as lifting the spirit of the reader to heights of greater knowledge, wisdom and faith regarding spiritual truth. Joanne Howe's book, *Biblical Answers to Catholic Questions*, is such a book.

The rarest kind of book is a book to be read. This is a book to be read not only by Catholics but also by everyone who is seeking Bible answers to the most important questions the human mind can pose. B.C. Goodpasture, former editor of the *Gospel Advocate*, wrote: "He who writes a good book may render mankind a greater service than he who amasses a fortune, wins a battle or founds an empire. Great books have been major forces in fashioning the lives and determining the destinies of men." Howe's books have had that kind of influence.

And now she has completed her third major work, another book that will without a doubt become a major force in making a difference in the lives of those who read it. Howe has taken a long journey in her life. From the time she gave up her father's religion to become a New Testament Christian until today, she has devoted her life to studying, teaching and bringing lost souls to Christ for salvation. She shares that adventure in this work, which is a culmination of her studies into the most important subjects found in the Bible.

The apostle Peter stated that God's "divine power has given to us all things that pertain to life and godliness, through the knowledge of Him who called us by glory and virtue" (2 Peter 1:3). That knowledge is provided by God's written Word (vv. 3-21). Howe's book emphasizes the necessity of going to the Bible for our wellspring of knowledge that we may be provided answers from the mind of God, spoken first by His Son and written down through the inspiration of the Holy Spirit by the apostles and prophets of the first century (John 14:24-26; 16:12-15; Hebrews 1:2; Ephesians 3:5).

I am grateful to Joanne Howe for taking the several years required to write and publish this book. It is a valuable tool for the serious-minded student of God's Word and those who hunger and thirst after the righteousness of God, which can be found only in Scripture. Through hundreds of scriptures, she presents and validates with great convincing power the truthfulness on which the Christian faith should be based because "faith comes by hearing, and hearing by the word of God" (Romans 10:17). My prayer and hope is that much fruit will be harvested for the kingdom of Christ and the glory of God through the circulating of this profitable presentation of the truth that makes us free in Christ.

Charles R. Williams
Academic Instructor
Amridge University

PREFACE

"Be diligent to present yourself approved to God, a worker who does not need to be ashamed, rightly dividing the word of truth" **(2 Timothy 2:15)**.

In 1971, after hours of counseling, study, worry and fear of betrayal to my faith as a Roman Catholic, I struggled with the decision I had to make in following the will of God as contained in the Bible. I thought back over the 19 years I had lived as a nun, fulfilling a vow I made to God at age 10 and serving Him in this capacity. As a third generation Catholic, I grew up loving the people of my Catholic faith – their heritage, their customs, their doctrines and, most especially, their rituals as a way of life. I believed and never questioned those in the hierarchy when told they spoke for God and their proclamations were ordained for me to follow to attain salvation.

During the Dark Ages, it was a crime for anyone to deviate from what was decreed by the hierarchy in Rome. The Roman church built up her religious power by absolute control over all who came under her rule. Many were burned at the stake for owning a Bible. I remember being horrified when learning of the price many believers paid for their search for truth. Whatever cost I had to pay should I leave my parents' religion was a sacrifice I was willing to make. My sincere desire to follow Christ led me to investigate the traditions and doctrines through my personal study of God's Word as presented in the Bible. I asked myself the following questions:

When did the Roman Catholic Church begin? Does the Roman Catholic Church have a legitimate claim on apostolic succession? Was Peter chosen to be the first Pope? Do I know the history and development of the doctrines of the Roman Catholic Church? Do these doctrines agree with the teachings of Christ? Are the sacraments of the Roman Catholic Church able to make me holy and acceptable to God? Does Catholicism teach that its doctrine and beliefs can lead me to heaven? Is Roman Catholicism the faith Christ would have me to believe and practice?

The more I read God's Word in an attempt to justify my Catholic beliefs, the more I realized God's truths held the answers to many of my questions and were in opposition to Catholic doctrines. I came to realize I could not earn God's favor and make myself acceptable to Him through an endless succession of various rituals, meritorious works and sacraments not ordained by God. I was confronted by an aching question from the depths of my heart: Should I leave my father's religion?

While reading the Douay Bible (my Catholic Bible), I gave serious consideration to a passage recorded in God's Word: "Beloved, do not believe every spirit, but test the spirits, whether they are of God; because many false prophets have gone out into the world" (1 John 4:1).

After months of study, prayer and all that is involved in the decision-making process, I left my Catholic faith, believing and accepting God's Word to be the only way, the only truth and the only life for me. God's teachings have equipped me for the life I now live and the eternity I hope to experience with God. My faith in the revelations of God's Word has deepened my love for my Lord and has strengthened the surrender of my heart and life to Him. It has lifted the blindness of my mind and heart and has carried me on an endless search for godly truths. I have a deeply settled peace in my soul because God's Word has given me confidence to be His ambassador, heralding His truths to a world of religious ignorance and false teachings. I stand with the apostle Paul when he said, "For I am not ashamed of the gospel of Christ, for it is the power of God to salvation for everyone who believes" (Romans 1:16).

As a result of my change of lifestyle and biblical beliefs, I wrote my first book, *A Change of Habit*. This book is my autobiography and my testimony to God's love, mercy and grace. It goes into greater detail on my reasons for entering the convent and why I left after 19 years of service.

My second book, *From Nun to Priest*, is a comparison of Catholic doctrines and biblical teachings. It has been a tremendous help to meeting the needs of many Roman Catholics and others seeking to understand God's Word versus the traditions of men.

Long ago as a young child, I learned about my Catholic faith through my study and memorization of the *Baltimore Catechism*. It presented a question and then gave the theological answer, minus scriptural references. Concerning the origin of another Catholic catechism (*Compendium: Catechism of the Catholic Church*), Ron Rhodes describes that it was "written under the direction of Cardinal Joseph Ratzinger, the present Pope now known as Benedict XVI, and was approved by Pope John Paul II in 1992. It is a statement of the Roman Catholic's faith and doctrines attested to or illumined by sacred scripture, apostolic tradition, and the Magisterium (the Catholic Church's teaching body)" (21).

The first lesson of the *Baltimore Catechism* contains questions and answers related to mankind's existence:

"1. Who made us?
God made us.

2. Who is God?
God is the Supreme Being, infinitely perfect, Who made all things and keeps them in existence.

3. Why did God make us?
God made us to show forth His goodness and to share with us His everlasting happiness in heaven" (9).

This question-and-answer method was used to educate me to the teachings of Catholicism and to give me a solid grounding on which to build my faith. This material was so strongly enforced by the nuns and the priests that even today I can quote the *Baltimore Catechism*. Catholicism was in my blood as a culture I inherited from my parents and grandparents. In other words, I was a "cradle Catholic."

I have chosen to use a similar format for this book. It is designed to become a biblical catechism for anyone seeking godly truths. Peter reminded us of our need to be ready to give a scriptural defense for our beliefs and traditions (1 Peter 3:15). Please note that not every question posed comes from the Catholic catechism, but these are included to address commonly held misunderstandings.

To understand what God wants us to believe and how to live those beliefs necessitates a knowledge of His Word. A biblical catechism for those Catholics seeking God's truths is long overdue in acquiring this knowledge. Sincere believers will often come to different opinions, thus formulating their own beliefs and conclusions. However, only God's Word holds the moral absolutes of who we are, what we need to believe and what road we need to take as we journey to our final destiny in eternity.

Since becoming a student of God's Word, I have come to realize that memorization of Scripture often becomes part of one's knowledge and life's application when understanding godly truths. In this biblical catechism, a question will be posed. Some questions will teach biblical doctrine while other questions will pertain to the doctrines and traditions taught by the hierarchy of the Roman Catholic Church. The answer that follows will come from the truth revealed by God's Holy Spirit in the Bible, using book, chapter and verse. In some sections, a comment will be made about a particular doctrine. If there is any catechism in the world, the Bible must be the standard for it.

As I prayed, planned and prepared to bring a biblical searchlight from God's Word for Catholics and others, it is my compassionate, loving and heartfelt belief that this book will bring the truths of God's wonderful gospel and His amazing grace to every seeking heart. The abundant life with God is ours for the choosing, for He will never force His teachings on us. We must choose them. Our faith is not just a matter of believing in God but also of trusting in His dependability to do what is right and to fulfill His promises. "[H]e who comes to God must believe that He is, and that He is a rewarder of those who diligently seek Him" (Hebrews 11:6).

This book will quickly help you find God's answers to legitimate questions and critical doctrines at the heart of Roman Catholicism. Your faith in God and His inspired Word can and will operate in you for your good and for God's glory.

In conclusion, I want you, the reader, to know that I love those in my former faith. My motivation for writing this book is based on the same desire that the apostle Paul had for his beloved people, the Jews, when he wrote these words for them: "Brethren, my heart's desire and prayer to God for Israel is that they may be saved. For I bear them witness that they have a zeal for God, but not according to knowledge" (Romans 10:1-2).

INTRODUCTION

Millions of sincere believing Catholics put their trust and beliefs in the Roman Catholic Church and her doctrines. They are convinced the Roman Catholic Church is the true church as established by Jesus Christ. Nevertheless, as will be shown in the following pages of this book, the gospel according to Rome is not the "good news" taught by Jesus in the Holy Scriptures and recorded for mankind's knowledge, nor is it the way to eternal salvation. The doctrines taught by Rome describe a different gospel – a gospel mixed with faith, traditions and works – as a way to gain salvation and acceptance before God.

The authority figures of the Roman Catholic Church believe and teach that the Word of God is not limited to the pages of the Bible. During the Second Vatican Council (1962–1965), documents titled *Dogmatic Constitution on Divine Revelation* reaffirmed the belief that Roman Catholic ecclesiastical authority was passed on by the apostles to other bishops in the churches of the first century and then to those in centuries that followed. This became known as "apostolic succession" (*Dogmatic Constitution on Divine Revelation* 7).

As years went by, the Roman Catholic Church began to add teachings based on what is now known as "Sacred Tradition." In order to substantiate their position in accepting the addition of tradition as the unwritten word of God, the Roman Catholic Church claims that the Bible is not the only guide of rule for faith and morals. The ecclesiastical authority totally rejects the belief in "*Sola Scriptura*," the teaching that the Bible alone is all we need for our spiritual authority. They stand firm on their conviction that doctrines instituted because of tradition are of the highest good for the Roman Catholic Church.

Consequently, the Bible and tradition are regarded as equal sources for spiritual authority and faith. Jesus condemned the scribes and the Pharisees of His day for following traditions above the Word of God. He was very emphatic when He said: "[I]n vain they worship Me, Teaching as doctrines the commandments of men'" (Mark 7:7; see also vv. 9, 13).

In Galatians, the apostle Paul showed that God does not recognize or authorize the rites and doctrines of Catholicism as the revealed and inspired gospel of Jesus Christ: "[I]f anyone preaches any other gospel to you than what you have received, let him be accursed" (1:9).

The more the teachings of Roman Catholicism are held under the microscope of the Scriptures, the greater the opportunities will be to communicate the gospel effectively to those Catholics who sincerely and earnestly seek godly truth. The apostle Peter reaffirmed the utmost necessity in accepting Scripture alone for faith and morals when he said: "[P]rophecy never came by the will of man, but holy men of God spoke as they were moved by the Holy Spirit" (2 Peter 1:21).

The teachings of these men did not use words that would falsify or destroy the message of Scripture. The message they delivered was by the inspiration and revelation of God's Holy Spirit.

In the book of Acts, we read of a group of people in a small town in Berea who were sincerely seeking truth. They received the Word of God with all readiness of mind and heart while searching the Scriptures daily to see whether these things were so.

"These were more fair-minded than those in Thessalonica, in that they received the word with all readiness, and searched the Scriptures daily to find out whether these things were so" (Acts 17:11).

As a student of God's revealed and inspired Word, I can identify with their seeking hearts. I search the Bible constantly for godly truth and the teachings of Jesus. My prayer is that those of my former people, Roman Catholics, will also search diligently the Scriptures presented in this book. I hope they also will come to the realization that the doctrines, church laws and rituals of Roman Catholicism are in direct opposition to biblical teachings.

BACK TO THE BASICS

I.

IDENTIFYING GOD

QUESTION #1:

How does God define Himself?

Catholic Response:

God is the "Creator of heaven and earth" (*Baltimore Catechism* 10). He made all things from nothing by His almighty power.

Biblical Response:

"And God said to Moses, 'I AM WHO AM.' And He said, 'Thus you shall say to the children of Israel, "I AM has sent me to you."' Moreover God said to Moses, "Thus you shall say to the children of Israel: 'The LORD God of your fathers, the God of Abraham, the God of Isaac, and the God of Jacob, has sent me to you. This is My name forever, and this is My memorial to all generations'" (Exodus 3:14-15).

QUESTION #2:

How does God explain His existence?

Catholic Response:

"We can know by our natural reason that there is a God, for natural reason tells us that the world we see about us could have been made only by a self-existing Being, all-wise and almighty" (*Baltimore Catechism* 16).

Biblical Response:

"Before the mountains were brought forth, or ever You had formed the earth and the world, Even from everlasting to everlasting, You are God" (Psalm 90:2).

"Remember the former things of old, For I am God, and there is no other; I am God, and there is none like Me, Declaring the end from the beginning, And from ancient times things that are not yet done, Saying, 'My counsel shall stand, And I will do all My pleasure'" (Isaiah 46:9-10).

"Now to the King eternal, immortal, invisible, to God who alone is wise, be honor and glory forever and ever" (1 Timothy 1:17).

QUESTION #3:

Can we know that God exists today?

Biblical Response:

"[T]urn … to the living God, who made the heaven, the earth, the sea, and all things that are in them, who in bygone generations allowed all nations to walk in their own ways. Nevertheless He did not leave Himself without witness, in that He did good, gave us rain from heaven and fruit-ful seasons, filling our hearts with food and gladness" (Acts 14:15-17).

QUESTION #4:

Who has given mankind the ability to know the truth about God?

Catholic Response:

"God has revealed these truths to us … He has made them known to certain persons, to be announced to their fellow men as the word of God. These persons chosen and sent by God are called 'witnesses' to Him" (*Baltimore Catechism* 16).

Biblical Response:

"For the wrath of God is revealed from heaven against all ungodliness and unrighteousness of men, who suppress the truth in unrighteousness, because what may be known of God is manifest in them, for God has shown it to them. For since the creation of the world His invisible attributes are clearly seen, being understood by the things that are made, even His eternal power and Godhead, so that they are without excuse" (Romans 1:18-20).

QUESTION #5:

What proofs do we have that there is only one God?

Catholic Response:

"God is the Supreme Being ... above all creatures, the self-existing and infinitely perfect Spirit" (*Baltimore Catechism* 13).

Biblical Response:

"I am God, and there is none like Me" (Isaiah 46:9).

QUESTION #6:

What are the characteristics of God as they are identified in the Bible?

Catholic Response:

"Some of the perfections of God are: God is eternal, all-good, all-knowing, all-present, and almighty." God also has intelligence, has power, has goodness, has no limitations, knows all things, can do all things, is all-good and is eternal (*Baltimore Catechism* 14-15).

Biblical Response:

God is self-existent (Genesis 1:1), eternal (Psalm 92), holy (Isaiah 6:3), unchangeable (Hebrews 13:8), just (Revelation 15:3), almighty (Revelation 19:6), all-knowing (Proverbs 5:21), present everywhere in spirit form (Psalm 139:7-12), love (John 3:16), and personally involved in His creation (Psalm 139:1-4).

QUESTION #7:

In what form does God exist?

Catholic Response:

God is a "self-existing and [an] infinitely perfect Spirit ... that has understanding and free will but no body, and will never die" (*Baltimore Catechism* 13).

Biblical Response:

The One God exists in three distinct persons: the Father, the Son and the Holy Spirit (Matthew 3:16-17).

Comment:

The biblically based orthodox doctrine of the Trinity has not been universally accepted at any time in history in what is broadly called Christendom. Yet we need to understand this fact because it ultimately shapes one's view of God. If I believe God is three separate persons, my worship of God then becomes polytheistic. If I think God is one Person, I divorce myself from the Bible and lose my faith-anchor for daily living. However, a biblical perception of the Trinity is essential for understanding the Scriptures. There are three persons in one: God the Father, the Son and the Holy Spirit. This unity was identified at the baptism of Jesus as recorded for our understanding in Matthew 3:16-17. Jesus also spoke of the Trinity being identified when one is baptized (Matthew 28:18-20).

QUESTION #8:

How does each person of the Godhead function?

Catholic Response:

"In God there are three divine persons – the Father, the Son, and the Holy Spirit. … By the blessed Trinity we mean one and the same God … The three divine Persons are really distinct from one another" (*Baltimore Catechism* 22-23).

Biblical Response:

Each person of God has a part in salvation.

"For God so loved the world that He gave His only begotten Son, that whoever believes in Him should not perish but have everlasting life" (John 3:16).

"[Jesus] humbled Himself and became obedient to the point of death, even the death of the cross" (Philippians 2:8).

"[W]hen He, the Spirit of truth, has come, He will guide you into all truth; for He will not speak on His own authority, but whatever He hears He will speak" (John 16:13).

II

IDENTIFYING JESUS CHRIST

QUESTION #1:

Who is Jesus Christ?

Catholic Response:

"The Son of God was conceived and made man by the power of the Holy Spirit in the womb of the Blessed Virgin Mary" (*Baltimore Catechism* 48).

Biblical Response:

Christ's arrival was foretold in the book of Isaiah that He would leave heaven to be born of a virgin. Eight biblical statements confirm His identity as the Son of God.

1. Christ would come through the seed of a woman: "[T]he LORD God said to the serpent: ... 'I will put enmity Between you and the woman, And between your seed and her Seed'" (Genesis 3:14-15).

2. He will be born of a virgin: "[T]he Lord Himself will give you a sign: Behold, the virgin shall conceive and bear a Son, and shall call His name Immanuel" (Isaiah 7:14).

3. The Savior will be born in Bethlehem: "But you, Bethlehem Ephrathah, Though you are little among the thousands of Judah, Yet out of you

shall come forth to Me The One to be Ruler in Israel" (Micah 5:2).

4. He performed genuine miracles that confirmed He is the Son of God (John 3:1-2).

   a. Christ fed the multitudes with "five loaves and two fish" (Matthew 14:14-19).

   b. Christ raised his friend Lazarus from the tomb (John 11:39-44).

   c. Christ walked on water (Matthew 14:25-33).

5. He became known as the world's greatest Teacher.

   a. Even his enemies reported that they had never heard a man speak like him: "And the Jews marveled saying, 'How does this Man know letters, having never studied?'" (John 7:15).

   b. "And so it was, when Jesus had ended these sayings, that the people were astonished at His teaching, for He taught them as one having authority, and not as the scribes" (Matthew 7:28-29).

6. Although Jesus was divine, He had taken on Him the form of a man: "And being found in appearance as a man, He humbled Himself and became obedient to the point of death, even the death of the cross" (Philippians 2:8).

7. Following His death on the cross, Christ was buried in the tomb (John 19:40-42), was raised on the first day of the week (Matthew 28:1-8) and ascended back to heaven (Acts 1:9).

8. "[Christ] is the image of the invisible God, the firstborn over all creation. For by Him all things were created that are in heaven and that are on earth, visible and invisible, whether thrones or dominions or principalities or powers. All things were created through Him and for Him. And He is before all things, and in Him all things consist" (Colossians 1:15-17).

QUESTION #2:

Why should we believe in Jesus Christ?

Catholic Response:

"The chief teaching of the Catholic Church about Jesus Christ is that He is God made man. ... Jesus Christ is God because He is the only Son of God, having the same divine nature as His Father" (*Baltimore Catechism* 46-47).

Biblical Response:

Jesus said: "I am the way, the truth, and the life. No one comes to the Father except through Me" (John 14:6).

Jesus also said: "You search the Scriptures, for in them you think you have eternal life; and these are they which testify of Me" (John 5:39).

QUESTION #3:

What part did Jesus Christ play in man's salvation?

Catholic Response:

"God did not abandon man after Adam fell into sin, but promised to send into the world a Savior to free man from his sins and to reopen to him the gates of heaven. ... The Savior of all men is Jesus Christ" (*Baltimore Catechism* 46).

Biblical Response:

"[Y]our iniquities have separated you from your God; And your sins have hidden His face from you" (Isaiah 59:2).

God "has saved us and called us with a holy calling, not according to our works, but according to His own purpose and grace which was given us in Christ Jesus before time began" (2 Timothy 1:9).

"[F]or all have sinned and fall short of the glory of God, being justified freely by His grace through the redemption that is in Christ Jesus, whom God set forth as a propitiation by His blood, through faith, to demonstrate His righteousness, because in His forbearance God had passed over the sins that were previously committed, to demonstrate at the present time His righteousness, that He might be just and the justifier of the one who has faith in Jesus" (Romans 3:23-26).

"Inasmuch then as the children have partaken of flesh and blood, He [Christ] Himself likewise shared in the same, that through death He might destroy him who had the power of death, that is the devil, and release those who through fear of death were all their lifetime subject to bondage. For indeed He does not give aid to angels, but He does give aid to the seed of Abraham. Therefore, in all things He had to be made like His brethren, that He might be a merciful and faithful High Priest in things pertaining to God, to make propitiation for the sins of the people" (Hebrews 2:14-17).

"For He [God] made Him [Jesus] who knew no sin to be sin for us, that we might become the righteousness of God in Him [Jesus]" (2 Corinthians 5:21).

Comment:

Before Christ came into the world, man's condition was one of alienation and separation from God. Mankind, by his sin, had severed his relationship with God. It took the death of Jesus Christ on the cross to restore the fractured relationship between God and mankind. Jesus suffered cruel scourging, (Matthew 27:26; Mark 15:15), mocking and mental torture (John 19:1-3) and was made to carry His wooden cross. His hands (or wrists) and feet (or ankles) were nailed to this wooden cross, and Christ hung there for six excruciating hours while priests, soldiers, curiosity-seekers and criminals all mocked him (Mark 15:25-37). Through His thirst, pain and humiliation, Jesus was thinking of each of us. This is the part that Christ played in mankind's salvation so that we could be admitted to the blessings of God's divine favor. The apostle Peter described it this way: "[Jesus] Himself bore our sins in His own body on the tree, that we, having died to sins, might live for righteousness – by whose stripes you were healed" (1 Peter 2:24).

III.

IDENTIFYING THE HOLY SPIRIT

QUESTION #1:
Who is the Holy Spirit?

Catholic Response:
"The Holy Spirit is God and the third Person of the Blessed Trinity. … The three divine Persons are perfectly equal to one another because all are one and the same God. … [T]his is a supernatural mystery" (*Baltimore Catechism* 23-24).

Biblical Response:
The Holy Spirit is an individual with a personality. "And I will pray the Father, and He will give you another Helper, that He may abide with you forever – the Spirit of truth, whom the world cannot receive, because it neither sees Him nor knows Him; but you know Him, for He dwells with you and will be in you" (John 14:16-17).

QUESTION #2:
What are the different names for God's Holy Spirit?

Biblical Response:
1. Holy Spirit: "Jesus, being filled with the Holy Spirit, returned from the Jordan and was led by the Spirit into the wilderness" (Luke 4:1).
2. Spirit of God: "For what man knows the things of a man except the spirit of the man which is in him? Even so no one knows the things of God except the Spirit of God" (1 Corinthians 2:11).
3. Helper: "But the Helper, the Holy Spirit, whom the Father will send in My name, He will teach you all things, and bring to your remembrance all things that I said to you" (John 14:26).
4. Spirit of Truth: "But when the Helper comes, whom I shall send to you from the Father, the Spirit of truth" (John 15:26).
5. Spirit of the Lord: "The Spirit of the LORD is upon Me, Because He has anointed Me To preach the gospel to the poor" (Luke 4:18).
6. Spirit of Christ: "Now if anyone does not have the Spirit of Christ, he is not His" (Romans 8:9).

QUESTION #3:
How does God's Holy Spirit function?

Catholic Response:

"The Holy Spirit dwells in the Church as the source of its life and sanctifies souls through the gift of grace" (*Baltimore Catechism* 60).

Biblical Response:
1. He can remind and teach: "But the Helper, the Holy Spirit, whom the Father will send in My name, He will teach you all things, and bring to your remembrance all things that I said to you" (John 14: 26).
2. He will bear witness: "But when the Helper comes, whom I shall send to you from the Father, the Spirit of truth who proceeds from the Father, He will testify of Me" (John 15:26).
3. He will disclose to you what is to come: "He will tell you things to come" (John 16:13).
4. He will give life: "He who raised Christ from the dead will also give life to your mortal bodies through His Spirit who dwells in you" (Romans 8:11).
5. He reveals and searches: "But it is written: 'Eye has not seen, nor ear heard, Nor have entered into the heart of man The things which

God has prepared for those who love Him.' But God has revealed them to us through His Spirit. For the Spirit searches all things, yes, the deep things of God. ... [N]o one knows the things of God except the Spirit of God" (1 Corinthians 2:9-11).

6. He promises: "[T]hat the blessing of Abraham might come upon the Gentiles in Christ Jesus, that we might receive the promise of the Spirit through faith" (Galatians 3:14).

7. He intercedes for our weaknesses: "Likewise the Spirit also helps in our weaknesses. For we do not know what we should pray for as we ought, but the Spirit Himself makes intercession for us with groanings which cannot be uttered. Now He who searches the hearts knows what the mind of the Spirit is, because He makes intercession for the saints according to the will of God" (Romans 8:26-27).

8. He anoints: "But you have an anointing from the Holy One, and you know all things" (1 John 2:20).

9. He fills us: "And do not be drunk with wine, in which is dissipation; but be filled with the [Holy] Spirit" (Ephesians 5:18).

10. He witnesses to us: "The Spirit Himself bears witness with our spirit that we are the children of God" (Romans 8:16).

11. He seals us: "And do not grieve the Holy Spirit of God, by whom you were sealed for the day of redemption" (Ephesians 4:30).

12. He convicts: "[I]f I depart, I will send Him [the Helper] to you. And when He has come, He will convict the world of sin, and of righteousness, and of judgment" (John 16:7-8).

QUESTION #4:

When did Christ promise the arrival of God's Holy Spirit, and to whom did He give this promise?

Biblical Response:

"These things I have spoken to you [the apostles], while being present with you. But the Helper, the Holy Spirit, whom the Father will send in My name, He will teach you all things, and bring to your remembrance all things that I said to you" (John 14:25-26).

"And you [apostles] also will bear witness, because you have been with Me from the beginning" (John 15:27).

QUESTION #5:

What are the important teachings given to us by God's Holy Spirit?

Catholic Response:

"The Bible is the written word of God, committed to His Church for the instruction and sanctification of mankind" (*Baltimore Catechism* 17).

Biblical Response:

"All Scripture is given by inspiration of God, and is profitable for doctrine, for reproof, for correction, for instruction in righteousness, that the man of God may be complete, thoroughly equipped for every good work" (2 Timothy 3:16-17).

Each of the divine examples of conversion in the book of Acts shows beyond doubt that the Holy Spirit converts individuals through the Word of God.

1. Large groups of believers: "Then those who gladly received his word were baptized; and that day about three thousand souls were added to them" (Acts 2:41); "[Many] of those who heard the word believed; and the number of the men came to be about five thousand" (4:4).
2. The Samaritans: "[T]hey believed Philip as he preached" (Acts 8:12).
3. Simon "also believed" (Acts 8:13).
4. The eunuch: "Philip ... preached Jesus to him ... and he baptized him" (Acts 8:35-38).
5. Saul of Tarsus: "[Y]ou will be told all things ... for you to do" (Acts 22:10).
6. Cornelius: "[W]ords by which you.... will be saved" (Acts 11:14).
7. Lydia "opened her heart to heed the things spoken by Paul" (Acts 16:14).
8. Jailer: "They spoke the word of the Lord to him" (Acts 16:32).
9. The Corinthians "hearing, believed and were baptized" (Acts 18:8).
10. The Bereans "received the word with all readiness, and searched the Scriptures daily" (Acts 17:11).
11. About 12 disciples: "When they heard this [Paul's teaching], they were baptized in the name of the Lord Jesus" (Acts 19:5).

Comment:

God's Word is the instrument or the tool through which the Holy Spirit tells us about God's will. The Holy Spirit is referred to numerous times throughout the Bible. He is sometimes called the Helper or Comforter (KJV). In theological circles, He may be called the Paraclete. The Spirit is not any less important than God the Father and God the Son. He is also God, and what He does for us is of tremendous importance. The truth in God's Word is the tool that converts a sinner and gives him the guidance he needs and advises him in "all things that pertain to life and godliness" (2 Peter 1:3).

QUESTION #6:

How are the teachings of the Holy Spirit and the teachings of Jesus connected?

Catholic Response:

"The Holy Spirit is the soul of the Catholic Church. He dwells in it to give it life. The life-blood of grace which flows through every living member of the Mystical Body of Christ comes from the Holy Spirit" (*Baltimore Catechism* 60).

Biblical Response:

"He who does not love Me does not keep my words; and the word which you hear is not Mine but the Father's who sent Me" (John 14:24).

"It is the Spirit who gives life; the flesh profits nothing. The words that I speak to you are spirit, and they are life" (John 6:63).

QUESTION #7:

What requirements did Jesus give for receiving God's Holy Spirit?

Biblical Response:

"Most assuredly, I say to you, unless one is born of water and the Spirit, he cannot enter the kingdom of God" (John 3:5).

QUESTION #8:

How is God's Holy Spirit involved in the new birth?

Biblical Response:

"[H]aving been born again, not of corruptible seed but incorruptible, through the word of God which lives and abides forever" (1 Peter 1:23).

QUESTION #9:

Why is the Word of God important in learning about the new birth?

Biblical Response:

"In Him you also trusted, after you heard the word of truth, the gospel of your salvation; in whom also, having believed, you were sealed with the Holy Spirit of promise" (Ephesians 1:13).

QUESTION #10:

Can an infant receive the Holy Spirit at baptism?

Biblical Response:

Scripture does not authorize infants to be baptized. A candidate for baptism must be taught accountability and understand the necessity to believe: "He who believes and is baptized will be saved" (Mark 16:16). One must repent of his sins and confess Jesus as his Lord and Savior. Only those individuals capable of believing, repenting, confessing and professing a desire to be baptized are acceptable candidates to Christ's invitation for the new birth (Matthew 28:19).

Comment:

Little children have an automatic entrance into the kingdom of heaven should they die. In Mark 10:14, Jesus said: "Let the little children come to Me, and do not forbid them; for of such is the kingdom of God." Scripture does not teach of a place called Limbo where unbaptized babies are sent. This is a man-made doctrine.

QUESTION #11:

What occurs when one receives the new birth?

Catholic Response:

"Baptism is the sacrament that gives our souls the new life of sanctifying grace by which we become children of God and heirs of heaven. … Baptism takes away original sin; and also actual sin and all the punishment due to them" (*Baltimore Catechism* 152).

Biblical Response:

"[D]o you not know that as many of us as were baptized into Christ

Jesus were baptized into His death? Therefore we were buried with Him through baptism into death, that just as Christ was raised from the dead by the glory of the Father, even so we also should walk in newness of life" (Romans 6:3-4).

Peter said: "Repent, and let every one of you be baptized in the name of Jesus Christ for the remission of sins; and you shall receive the gift of the Holy Spirit" (Acts 2:38).

QUESTION #12:
Why is it necessary to be baptized (immersed)?

Biblical Response:
Jesus said in Mark 16:16: "He who believes and is baptized will be saved."

QUESTION #13:
How is baptism administered?

Catholic Response:
"At its FIRST BIRTH a child has sin on its soul. Going under the water in Baptism, the child dies to sin and is buried with Christ. Coming up out of the water (SECOND BIRTH) symbolizes rising with Christ to the new life of grace ... (This is also symbolized, though not so expressly, when the water is only poured on the person being baptized.) ... I would give Baptism by pouring ordinary water on the forehead of the person to be baptized" (*Baltimore Catechism* 151-153).

Biblical Response:
In Matthew 3:16 we read: "Jesus came up immediately from the water." In Acts 8:38, the one baptized "went down into the water." In Colossians 2:12 we read that when one is baptized, he or she "is buried ... in baptism."

QUESTION #14:
What changes occur when one is baptized?

Biblical Response:
Baptism changes our relationship with God. "For as many of you as were baptized into Christ have put on Christ" (Galatians 3:27).

IV.

IDENTIFYING MAN

QUESTION #1:
What is man?

Catholic Response:
"Man is a creature composed of body and soul, and made to the image and likeness of God ... This likeness to God is chiefly in the soul" (*Baltimore Catechism* 31).

Biblical Response:
"What is man that You are mindful of him ... ? For You have made him a little lower than the angels" (Psalm 8:4-5).

QUESTION #2:
What occurred when God created man?

Biblical Response:
"So God created man in His own image; in the image of God He created him; male and female He created them" (Genesis 1:27). All humans share some of God's characteristics.

QUESTION #3:
Why did God create man?

Biblical Response:
1. God lovingly created man in order to glorify Him (1 Corinthians 10:31).
2. Mankind finds meaning in life by investing in God's eternal values (Matthew 6:33).
3. Each of us has an eternal destiny with God if we exercise our faith and offer our obedience to His Son, Jesus Christ (1 Peter 1:3-4).

QUESTION #4:
What did God form in man?

Biblical Response:
"Thus says the LORD, who stretches out the heavens, lays the foundation of the earth, and forms the spirit of man within him" (Zechariah 12:1).

"Thus, says the LORD who made you And formed you from the womb, who will help you: 'Fear not'" (Isaiah 44:2).

QUESTION #5:
During man's lifetime, what keeps him alive? What happens to his body at death?

Biblical Response:
"For this corruptible must put on incorruption, and this mortal must put on immortality. So when this corruptible has put on incorruption, and this mortal has put on immortality, then shall be brought to pass the saying that is written: 'Death is swallowed up in victory'" (1 Corinthians 15:53-54).

"Then the dust will return to the earth as it was, And the spirit will return to God who gave it" (Ecclesiastes 12:7).

QUESTION #6:
What must each person face after death?

Catholic Response:
"The judgment which will be passed on all men immediately after the

general resurrection is called the general judgment. ... The judgment which will be passed on each on of us immediately after death is called the particular judgment. ... Although everyone is judged immediately after death, it is fitting that there be a general judgment in order that the justice, wisdom, and mercy of God may be glorified in the presence of all. ... [This judgment is] a public declaration and manifestation of the sentences or rewards already given or made in the particular judgment" (*Baltimore Catechism* 89).

Biblical Response:

After death, each person will stand before God to be judged personally and to give an account of his or her life. "And as it is appointed for man to die once, but after this the judgment" (Hebrews 9:27).

"For we must all appear before the judgment seat of Christ, that each one may receive the things done in the body, according to what he has done, whether good or bad" (2 Corinthians 5:10).

QUESTION #7:

What is our purpose in life?

Catholic Response:

"God made us to show forth His goodness and to share with us His everlasting happiness in heaven" (*Baltimore Catechism* 9).

Biblical Response:

"Let your light so shine before men, that they may see your good works and glorify your Father in heaven" (Matthew 5:16).

"Or do you not know that your body is the temple of the Holy Spirit who is in you, whom you have from God, and you are not your own? For you were brought at a price; therefore glorify God in your body and in your spirit, which are God's" (1 Corinthians 6:19-20).

"For we are His workmanship, created in Christ Jesus for good works, which God prepared beforehand that we should walk in them" (Ephesians 2:10).

QUESTION #8:

What determines our eternal destiny?

Catholic Response:

"The rewards or punishments appointed for men after the particular judgment are heaven, purgatory, or hell. ... Those are punished for a time in purgatory who die in the state of grace but are guilty of venial sin, or have not fully satisfied for the temporal punishment due to their sins. ... Purgatory is God's hospital for souls, where those who do not love God enough to enter heaven are cured by fire" (*Baltimore Catechism* 90).

Biblical Response:

Our actions on earth determine our eternal destiny. We can expect eternal life or everlasting destruction. "When the Son of Man comes in all His glory, and all the holy angels with Him, then He will sit on the throne of His glory. All the nations will be gathered before Him, and He will separate them one from another, as a shepherd divides his sheep from the goats. And He will set the sheep on His right hand, but the goats on the left. Then the King will say to those on His right hand, 'Come, you blessed of My Father, inherit the kingdom prepared for you from the foundation of the world' " (Matthew 25:31-34).

Comment:

Death is the ultimate personal experience. No one knows what others have felt at death. No one really knows death except Jesus who has overcome it. Death is actually a gift from God. His Word has given us very specific evidence about heaven and hell; it also tells us how to select one or the other. After Christ's second coming, the spirits of people in Paradise will be reunited for eternity with a body glorious and indestructible in heaven. On the other hand, the Bible describes hell as a place where "the fire ... shall never be quenched" (Mark 9:43), where a lake of fire burns with brimstone (Revelation 19:20). Hell will be a place of eternal darkness – a place where everyone and everything is separated from God forever. Jesus never minced words. He described hell as a place where there will be "weeping and gnashing of teeth" (Matthew 8:12; 22:13). The Bible tells us that God is just. Life after death becomes a place for complete justice because God's justice will certainly be revealed in all its magnificence and holiness in the afterlife (Psalm 9:7-8).

V.

FAITH

QUESTION #1:
What is faith?

Catholic Response:
"The theological virtue by which we believe all that God has revealed, and the body of truths which we believe" (*Baltimore Catechism* 246).

Biblical Response:
"Now faith is the substance of things hoped for, the evidence of things not seen" (Hebrews 11:1).

QUESTION #2:
How do we receive faith?

Biblical Response:
"So then faith comes by hearing, and hearing by the word of God" (Romans 10:17).

"For by grace you have been saved through faith, and that not of yourselves; it is the gift of God, not of works, lest anyone should boast" (Ephesians 2:8-9).

QUESTION #3:

Why is faith not a matter of one's opinion?

Biblical Response:

"If anyone speaks, let him speak as the oracles of God" (1 Peter 4:11).
"For we walk by faith, not by sight" (2 Corinthians 5:7).

QUESTION #4:

In whom should we place our faith?

Biblical Response:

"So Jesus answered and said to them, 'Have faith in God. For assuredly I say to you, whoever says to this mountain, "Be removed and be cast into the sea," and does not doubt in his heart, but believes that those things he says will be done, he will have whatever he says. Therefore I say to you, whatever things you ask when you pray, believe that you will receive them, and you will have them'" (Mark 11:22-24).

QUESTION #5:

What is the blessing of having faith in God?

Biblical Response:

"Though now you do not see Him [Jesus Christ], yet believing, you rejoice with joy inexpressible and full of glory, receiving the end of your faith – the salvation of your souls" (1 Peter 1:8-10).

"You will keep him in perfect peace, Whose mind is stayed on You, Because he trusts in You" (Isaiah 26:3).

QUESTION #6:

How important are faith and trust to God?

Biblical Response:

"But without faith it is impossible to please Him, for he who comes to God must believe that He is, and that He is a rewarder of those who diligently seek Him" (Hebrews 11:6).

"But he who puts his trust in Me shall possess the land, And shall inherit My holy mountain" (Isaiah 57:13).

"Trust in the LORD with all your heart, And lean not on your own understanding; In all your ways acknowledge Him, And He shall direct your paths" (Proverbs 3:5-6).

QUESTION #7:
How did John the Baptist express his faith when he saw Christ?

Biblical Response:
"John saw Jesus coming toward him, and said, 'Behold! The Lamb of God who takes away the sin of the world!' " (John 1:29).

QUESTION #8:
What is biblical faith built upon?

Biblical Response:
"Blessed are those who have not seen and yet have believed" (John 20:29).

QUESTION #9:
Why did Jesus compare faith to a mustard seed?

Biblical Response:
"And the apostles said to the Lord, 'Increase our faith.' So the Lord said, 'If you have faith as a mustard seed, you can say to this mulberry tree, "Be pulled up by the roots and be planted in the sea," and it would obey you'" (Luke 17:5-6).

QUESTION #10:
Who is the author and finisher of our faith?

Biblical Response:
"Therefore we also, since we are surrounded by so great a cloud of witnesses, let us lay aside every weight, and the sin which so easily ensnares us, and let us run with endurance the race that is set before us, looking to Jesus, the author and the finisher of our faith" (Hebrews 12:1-2).

QUESTION #11:

What is the one important gift we receive when we become born of God?

Biblical Response:

"For whatever is born of God overcomes the world. And this is the victory that has overcome the world – our faith" (1 John 5:4).

QUESTION #12:

Where does conscience come from, and does it have anything to do with faith?

Biblical Response:

"([F]or not the hearers of the law are just in the sight of God, but the doers of the law will be justified; for when Gentiles, who do not have the law, by nature do the things in the law, these, although not having the law, are a law to themselves, who show the work of the law written in their hearts, their conscience also bearing witness, and between themselves their thoughts accusing or else excusing them)" (Romans 2:13-15).

Comment:

God created within mankind's nature a moral consciousness of what is right or wrong. Merely knowing God's truths and not obeying His commandments is unacceptable before God. Having obedient faith and accepting God's Son, Jesus, makes one righteous and justified in the sight of God.

VI.

THE BIBLE

QUESTION #1:
What is the Bible?

Catholic Response:

"The Bible is the written word of God, committed to His Church for the instruction and sanctification of mankind" (*Baltimore Catechism* 17).

"We can know the true meaning of the Bible from the teaching authority of the Catholic Church, which has received from Jesus Christ the right and duty to teach and to explain all that God has revealed" (*Baltimore Catechism* 19).

Biblical Response:

"[T]he Holy Scriptures … are able to make you wise for salvation through faith which is in Christ Jesus. All Scripture is given by inspiration of God, and is profitable for doctrine, for reproof, for correction, for instruction in righteousness, that the man of God may be complete, thoroughly equipped for every good work" (2 Timothy 3:15-17).

"Your [God's] word is a lamp to my feet And a light to my path" (Psalm 119:105).

"For the word of God is living and powerful, and sharper than any two-edged sword, piercing even to the division of soul and spirit, and of joints and marrow, and is a discerner of the thoughts and intents of the heart" (Hebrews 4:12).

Comment:

The Bible is a unique library written by approximately 40 different men who lived in different centuries and different countries and were from different walks of life. These men were guided by God's Holy Spirit. They wrote 66 books over a period of 1,500 years. The Bible is divided into the Old Testament (39 books) and the New Testament (27 books).

Old Testament Books (39)

Books of the Law (6)

1. Genesis – a record of creation, Adam and Eve, and their descendants following the lineage of Abraham, Isaac and Jacob
2. Exodus – The Israelites leave Egypt, and the Law is given to them.
3. Leviticus – the requirements for priestly service
4. Numbers – Israel in the desert
5. Deuteronomy – the principles of the Law with its warnings; the death of Moses
6. Joshua – the conquest of Canaan

Books of History (11)

1. Judges – leaders who freed the Israelites from their oppressors
2. Ruth – family loyalty and faith
3. 1 Samuel – the end of the judges and the reign of King Saul
4. 2 Samuel – the reign of David
5. 1 Kings – reign of Solomon; division of the kingdom; prophet Elijah
6. 2 Kings – the fall of Israel (northern kingdom) to Assyria and the fall of Judah (southern kingdom) to Babylon
7. 1 Chronicles – David's reign as king
8. 2 Chronicles – Solomon; construction of the temple; record of the kings
9. Ezra – Exiles rebuild the temple.
10. Nehemiah – rebuilding the wall
11. Esther – Jews are saved from the massacre in Persia.

Books of Poetry (5)

1. Job – the problems of suffering
2. Psalms – Israel's songbook
3. Proverbs – wise sayings by Solomon
4. Ecclesiastes – the futility of life without trust in God
5. Song of Solomon – the wonder of physical love

Books of Prophecy (17)

1. Isaiah – Israel and Judah to fall; the remnant; predictions of the coming Messiah
2. Jeremiah – the effort to warn of the fall of Jerusalem and Judah; Babylonian captivity predicted
3. Lamentations – mourning for Jerusalem in ruins
4. Ezekiel – visions of Jerusalem and the future
5. Daniel – foretells world empires and the Messianic kingdom
6. Hosea – God's love and Israel's infidelity
7. Joel – judgment for that age and the future coming of the Holy Spirit
8. Amos – wickedness, destruction and restoration
9. Obadiah – punishment of Edom
10. Jonah – obedience and love
11. Micah – downfall of Israel and Judah and the coming Messiah
12. Nahum – fall of Nineveh foretold
13. Habakkuk – invasion of Judah and the fall of Babylon; faith in God
14. Zephaniah – the wrath of God upon nations followed by a time of acceptance by men from all nations
15. Haggai – exhortations to build the temple; God's future temple
16. Zechariah – rebuilding the temple; prophesies of a greater future temple and the coming of the Messiah and His kingdom
17. Malachi – rebuke for spiritual decay; judgment; day of the Lord

New Testament Books (27)

Biography of Jesus Christ (4)

1. Matthew – Jesus' fulfillment of Scripture as the Messiah
2. Mark – emphasizes Jesus as a servant to His people
3. Luke – the saving ministries of Jesus in His life and death
4. John – Jesus is portrayed as Lord and God.

History (1)

1. Acts – the spread of Christianity through the power of the Holy Spirit

Letters (21)

1. Romans – Righteousness with God is given to those who have faith in Jesus Christ.
2. 1 Corinthians – first letter by the apostle Paul to the church at Corinth; addresses congregational problems
3. 2 Corinthians – The Christian's ministry is commissioned by Christ and empowered by the Holy Spirit.
4. Galatians – Christians trust in Jesus Christ alone, not in their own ability to keep the law or do good works.
5. Ephesians – focuses on God's masterpiece: the church
6. Philippians – Knowing Jesus Christ brings joy.
7. Colossians – declares the supremacy of Christ as the head of the church
8. 1 Thessalonians – The coming of Christ is our true hope.
9. 2 Thessalonians – encourages Christians to stand firm
10. 1 Timothy – Christians must act with godly character.
11. 2 Timothy – Be committed to the teachings of God.
12. Titus – Sound doctrine is necessary for sound teaching.
13. Philemon – All Christians who have repented are brothers in Christ.
14. Hebrews – Christ is superior to the Old Covenant.
15. James – Good works are the evidence of genuine faith.
16. 1 Peter – hope for suffering believers
17. 2 Peter – warning to Christians about false teachers
18. 1 John – fellowship with Jesus and other believers
19. 2 John – encouragement to remain faithful to the truth
20. 3 John – Be committed to the truth of the Gospels.
21. Jude – Christians are soldiers in spiritual warfare.

Prophecy (1)

1. Revelation – prophecy of Christ's return to destroy all evil and the triumph of heaven

QUESTION #2:

Who wrote the Bible?

Catholic Response:

"[I]ts principal author is God, though it was written by men whom God enlightened and moved to write all those things, that He wished to be written. ... Inspiration is a force that God puts into a man so that he can write what God wants him to write. ... though he uses his own language, his own style and his own writing skill. The power of inspiration keeps the writer from making a mistake" (*Baltimore Catechism* 17).

Biblical Response:

"[H]oly men of God spoke as they were moved by the Holy Spirit" (2 Peter 1:21).

Jesus said: "For I have not spoken on My own authority; but the Father who sent Me gave Me a command, what I should say and what I should speak" (John 12:49).

"Now we have received, not the spirit of the world, but the Spirit who is from God, that we might know the things that have been freely given to us by God. These things we also speak, not in words which man's wisdom teaches but which the Holy Spirit teaches, comparing spiritual things with spiritual" (1 Corinthians 2:12-13).

QUESTION #3:

Why was the Bible written?

Biblical Response:

The purpose of the Bible is to reveal God, Christ, man, sin, salvation, the church, the necessity of being obedient to God's Word and man's eternity.

"The heavens declare the glory of God; And the firmament shows His handiwork" (Psalm 19:1).

"For since, in the wisdom of God, the world through wisdom did not know God, it pleased God through the foolishness of the message preached to save those who believe" (1 Corinthians 1:21).

"Grace and peace be multiplied to you in the knowledge of God and of Jesus our Lord, as His divine power has given to us all things that pertain unto life and godliness, through the knowledge of Him who called us by glory and virtue" (2 Peter 1:2-3).

"All Scripture is given by the inspiration of God, and is profitable for doctrine, for reproof, for correction, for instruction in righteousness, that the man of God may be complete, thoroughly equipped for every good work" (2 Timothy 3:16-17).

"Not everyone who says to Me, 'Lord, Lord,' shall enter the kingdom of heaven, but he who does the will of My Father in heaven" (Matthew 7:21).

"And if anyone hears My words and does not believe, I do not judge him; for I did not come to judge the world but to save the world. He who rejects Me, and does not receive My words, has that which judges him – the word that I have spoken will judge him in the last day" (John 12:47-48).

"[T]he gospel which was preached by me is not according to man. For I neither received it from man, nor was I taught it, but it came through the revelation of Jesus Christ" (Galatians 1:11-12).

QUESTION #4:
What is the canon of the Bible?

Comment:

The canon of the Bible consists of the Old Testament and the New Testament. These 66 books were written by about 40 individuals and are divided into three dispensations:

1. The Patriarchal Dispensation – The first period of time began with Abraham and ended with the giving of the Mosaic Law.
2. The Mosaic Dispensation – This second period began with Moses, who received the first written covenant from God (the Ten Commandments), and ended when Christ died on the cross.
3. The Christian Dispensation – This third period began with the death of Christ, nailing the covenant of the Ten Commandments to the cross (Colossians 2:14). The church was born on the Day of Pentecost following the resurrection of our Lord in the city of Jerusalem. Then a new covenant began (Hebrews 10:9-10).

The English word "canon" came to be known as a standard or rule. When applied to the Bible, it denotes a list of books received as Holy Scripture. These "canonical books" are regarded as having divine authority and make up the Bible. The Bible's divine authority is based on its inspiration and its canonicity. No church council, by its decrees, can make the books of the Bible authoritative. Jesus and His apostles quoted from this distinctive body of authoritative writings – the Law of Moses, the prophets and the psalms from the Old Testament – with the words "it is written," which means that it stands firmly written and is indisputably true. In Luke 24:44 Jesus said: "These are the words which I spoke to you while I was still with you, that all things must be fulfilled which were written in the Law of Moses and the Prophets and the Psalms concerning Me."

"When the church was established, there was no thought of a New Testament. Over a period of time, inspired men began to put in writing divine regulations, both for the churches and for individuals. These writings were held in high esteem, and by the end of the second century, Christians believed that a guiding providence revealed and inspired the canon of the New Testament" (Boettner 103).

QUESTION #5:

Has anyone been given the authority to interpret, add or take away the messages and teachings in the Bible?

Biblical Response:

Jesus sent His apostles out to represent Him, to bear His authority, and to teach in His name, saying: "[H]e who receives whomever I send receives Me; and he who receives Me receives Him who sent Me" (John 13:20).

"Paul, an apostle (not from men nor through man, but through Jesus Christ and God the Father who raised Him from the dead)" (Galatians 1:1).

Jesus said: "These things I have spoken to you while being present with you. But the Helper, the Holy Spirit, whom the Father will send in My name, He will teach you all things, and bring to your remembrance all things that I said to you" (John 14:25-26).

"If anyone speaks, let him speak as the oracles of God" (1 Peter 4:11).

"Whoever transgresses and does not abide in the doctrine of Christ does not have God" (2 John 1:9).

"And Jesus came and spoke to them, saying, 'All authority has been given to Me in heaven and on earth. Go therefore and make disciples of all the nations' " (Matthew 28:18-19).

"You shall not add in the word which I command you, nor take from it" (Deuteronomy 4:2).

QUESTION #6:
Does the Bible contradict itself?

Catholic Response:
"There are no errors or mistakes in the Bible. All that is there is truth" (*Baltimore Catechism* 17).

Biblical Response:
"I will raise up for them a Prophet like you from among their brethren, and will put My words in His mouth, and He shall speak to them all that I command Him. And it shall be that whoever will not hear My words, which He speaks in My name, I will require it of him" (Deuteronomy 18:18-19).

"All Scripture is given by inspiration of God, and is profitable for doctrine, for reproof, for correction, for instruction in righteousness, that the man of God may be complete, thoroughly equipped for every good work" (2 Timothy 3:16-17).

QUESTION #7:
Why is it important to know and understand the Scriptures?

Biblical Response:
The apostle Paul appealed to Timothy to follow Scripture when he said: "[F]rom childhood you have known the Holy Scriptures, which are able to make you wise for salvation" (2 Timothy 3:15).

"I found it necessary to write to you exhorting you to contend earnestly for the faith which was once for all delivered to the saints" (Jude 1:3).

"Let your speech always be with grace, seasoned with salt, that you may know how you ought to answer each one" (Colossians 4:6).

The Bible is the perfect guide to knowing and understanding the will of God. Jesus promised, the Spirit "will guide you into all truth" (John 16:13).

"[T]he Spirit who is from God, [is given] that we might know the things that have been freely given to us by God" (1 Corinthians 2:12).

"Grace and peace be multiplied to you in the knowledge of God and of Jesus our Lord, as His divine power has given to us all things that pertain to life and godliness, through the knowledge of Him who called us by glory and virtue" (2 Peter 1:2-3).

QUESTION #8:
Why do we not all see the Bible alike?

Comment:

Jesus prayed for unity, and the apostle Paul pleaded for the same. This unity of understanding has not occurred for the following reasons:

1. Some believe that the Bible cannot be understood and that it is beyond human comprehension. Jesus taught:
   a. "Not everyone who says to Me, 'Lord, Lord,' shall enter the kingdom of heaven, but he who does the will of My Father in heaven" (Matthew 7:21).
   b. "But God be thanked that though you were slaves of sin, yet you obeyed from the heart that form of doctrine to which you were delivered" (Romans 6:17).
2. Some believe that God never intended for us to understand the Bible, and others think that it does not matter if we understand biblical teachings the same. What does God say? "Be diligent to present yourself approved to God, a worker who does not need to be ashamed, rightly dividing the word of truth" (2 Timothy 2:15).
3. Some hold onto religious beliefs based on their denomination, their creeds and the influence of their parents. Jesus said: "He who loves father or mother more than Me is not worthy of Me. And he who loves son or daughter more than me is not worthy of Me" (Matthew 10:37).
4. "Therefore do not be unwise, but understand what the will of the Lord is" (Ephesians 5:17).

QUESTION #9:
Are the stories of the Bible fact or fiction?

Biblical Response:

In the last book of the New Testament, God said: "For I testify to every-one who hears the words of the prophecy of this book: If anyone adds to these things, God will add to him the plagues that are written in this book; and if anyone takes away from the words of the book of this prophecy, God shall take away his part from the Book of Life, from the holy city, and from the things which are written in this book" (Revelation 22:18-19).

QUESTION #10:
Who will be our judge when we stand before God?

Biblical Response:
"He who rejects Me, and does not receive My words, has that which judges him – the word that I have spoken will judge him in the last day" (John 12:48).

"For if we sin willfully after we have received the knowledge of the truth, there no longer remains a sacrifice for sins, but a certain fearful expectation of judgment, and fiery indignation which will devour the adversaries" (Hebrews 10:26-27). "It is a fearful thing to fall into the hands of the living God" (v. 31).

"While he [Peter] was still speaking, behold, a bright cloud overshadowed them; and suddenly a voice came out of the cloud, saying, 'This is my beloved Son, in whom I am well pleased. Hear Him!' " (Matthew 17:5).

QUESTION #11:
What is the Apocrypha? Should these books be in the canon of the Bible? Why or why not?

Comment:
The word "apocrypha" means "hidden things" and consists of 15 books that are a collection of ancient Jewish writings from about 300 B.C. to A.D. 100. Some of the writings have come to be regarded as inspired scripture in the theology of the Roman Catholic Church. The Apocrypha was never declared authoritative scripture until the Council of Trent (A.D. 1546). Bishop Damasus (near the close of the 4th century) commissioned Jerome to write the Latin version as the official Bible of the Roman Catholic Church known as the "Vulgate" (meaning common). The Council of Trent in 1546 decreed: "If anyone receives not, as sacred and canonical, the said books entire with all their parts, as they are contained in the Latin Vulgate edition, let him be anathema!"

The Apocryphal books were added to the Old Testament in the Catholic Bible because of the Protestant Reformation. The reformers of the Protestant Reformation questioned the canonical authenticity of these books and disagreed with the doctrines taken from the Apocryphal books. The Catholic doctrine of Purgatory and praying for the dead were challenged, and Roman scholars found doctrinal support in 2 Maccabees 12:40-45. The Vatican Council of 1870 (the same council that set forth the infallibility of the Pope when he speaks on faith and morals) declared once again that these Apocryphal books are without error. "[A]ccording to the Council of Trent, the Scriptures are and mean what the church says. Yet Rome, which in such matters claims infallibility, cannot make the fallible Apocrypha infallible" (Lightfoot 170).

QUESTION #12:

What Apocryphal writings have been added to the Old Testament in Roman Catholic Bibles?

Catholic Response:

Roman Catholic Bibles (e.g., Douay Bible) include 12 Apocryphal writings. Among them are seven Apocryphal books (called Deuterocanonical books by Catholics): Tobias (also called Tobit), Judith, Wisdom (also called Wisdom of Solomon), Sirach (also called Ecclesiasticus), Baruch, 1 Machabees (also spelled Maccabees) and 2 Machabees. (The variations in parenthesis differ from the names listed in the *Baltimore Catechism* on page 18.) Along with the seven Apocryphal books, Roman Catholic Bibles include five Apocryphal writings within those and other Old Testament books: Letter of Jeremiah (Baruch 6), additions to the book of Esther, Prayer of Azariah (Daniel 3:24-90), Susanna (Daniel 13), and Bel and the Dragon (Daniel 14).

Biblical Response:

Moses warned against adding to the Word of God when he said: "You shall not add to the word which I command you, nor take from it, that you may keep the commandments of the LORD your God which I command you" (Deuteronomy 4:2).

Jesus and His apostles never quoted from the Apocrypha because they did not regard those books as Scripture. In John 10:35, Jesus proclaimed the infallibility of the Scriptures when He spoke to those who were about to stone Him: "The Scripture cannot be broken." He also spoke to the Sadducees, confirming the importance of following Scripture: "You are mistaken, not knowing the Scriptures" (Matthew 22:29). When Jesus appeared to His apostles after His resurrection, He used the Scriptures: "And beginning at Moses and all the Prophets, He expounded to them in all the Scriptures the things concerning Himself" (Luke 24:27).

The apostle Peter, speaking of the Old Testament prophets, stated: "[F]or prophecy never came by the will of man, but holy men of God spoke as they were moved by the Holy Spirit" (2 Peter 1:21). The Old Testament was given to the Jews, and they never recognized the books of the Apocrypha.

QUESTION #13:
Did the Roman Catholic Church write the Bible?

Biblical Response:
"All authority has been given to Me in heaven and on earth. Go therefore and make disciples of all the nations, baptizing them in the name of the Father and of the Son and of the Holy Spirit, teaching them to observe all things that I have commanded you" (Matthew 28:18-20).

"You are mistaken, not knowing the Scriptures" (Matthew 22:29).

Comment:
The Roman Catholic Church did not exist before the message, and the teachings were given in God's revealed and inspired Word.

QUESTION #14:
Are we to follow the Bible or tradition?

Comment:
The Roman Catholic Church agrees that the Bible is the inspired Word of God, but Catholics also believe in two sources of authority – Scripture and tradition. They teach that Scripture is to be supplemented by the church fathers' writings, council pronouncements and papal dogmas. In some cases, the Catholic Church sees tradition as superior to Scripture. The Council of Trent in 1546 declared that the Word of

God is contained in both Scripture and tradition and both are of equal authority. This dogma was reaffirmed by the Second Vatican Council in 1962 (John H. Armstrong 113).

Biblical Response:
Jesus condemned and rebuked those who followed traditions rather than Scripture when He said:

1. "For laying aside the commandment of God, you hold the tradition of men … [Y]ou reject the commandment of God, that you may keep your tradition … making the word of God of no effect through your tradition which you have handed down" (Mark 7:8-13).

2. "He answered and said to them, 'Why do you also transgress the commandment of God because of your tradition?'" (Matthew 15:3). "[Y]ou have made the commandment of God of no effect by your tradition" (v. 6). "'And in vain they worship Me, Teaching as doctrines the commandments of men'" (v. 9).

3. The apostle Paul gave clear warning when he said: "Beware lest anyone cheat you through philosophy and empty deceit, according to the tradition of men, according to the basic principles of the world, and not according to Christ" (Colossians 2:8).

4. We must prove all things by the Word of God. "Do not despise prophecies. Test all things; hold fast what is good" (1 Thessalonians 5:20-21).

VII.

SIN

S in is defined as an offense or the condition of being guilty of continued offense "against God, religion, or good morals" (*Webster's* 1337). *Cruden's Concordance* defines sin as "any thought, word, action, omission, or desire, contrary to the law of God" (662).

QUESTION #1:
What is sin?

Catholic Response:
There are three categories of sin: original sin, mortal sin and venial sin. "On account of the sin of Adam, we, his descendants, come into the world deprived of sanctifying grace and inherit his punishment ... This sin in us is called original sin. ... This sin is called original because it comes down to us through our origin, or descent, from Adam." Mortal sin "is a grievous offense against the law of God," and venial sin "is a less serious offense against the law of God" (*Baltimore Catechism* 34, 40-41).

Biblical Response:

"Whosoever commits sin also commits lawlessness, and sin is lawlessness" (1 John 3:4).

"All unrighteousness is sin, and there is sin not leading to death" (1 John 5:17).

"Therefore, to him who knows to do good and does not do it, to him it is sin" (James 4:17).

The Bible does not address sin as being "original," "venial" or "mortal." People with sin of any nature, whether great or small, will not enter the gates of heaven. Only those whose names "are written in the Lamb's Book of Life" will enter the gates of heaven (Revelation 21:27).

QUESTION #2:

When did sin enter the world, and what are the results?

Biblical Response:

"Therefore, just as through one man [Adam] sin entered the world, and death through sin, and thus death spread to all men, because all sinned – (For until the law sin was in the world, but sin is not imputed when there is no law. Nevertheless death reigned from Adam to Moses, even over those who had not sinned according to the likeness of the transgression of Adam, who is a type of Him who was to come [Jesus]" (Romans 5:12-14).

QUESTION #3:

Does a person inherit sin at birth?

Biblical Response:

A person's spirit is pure at birth; sin cannot be inherited. "The soul who sins shall die. The son shall not bear the guilt of the father, nor the father bear the guilt of the son. The righteousness of the righteous shall be upon himself, and the wickedness of the wicked shall be upon himself" (Ezekiel 18:20).

QUESTION #4:

When does a person become a sinner?

Biblical Response:

"Let no one say when he is tempted, 'I am tempted by God'; for God cannot be tempted by evil, nor does He Himself tempt anyone. But each one is tempted when he is drawn away by his own desires and enticed. Then, when desire has conceived, it gives birth to sin; and sin, when it is full-grown, brings forth death" (James 1:13-15).

"Do you not know that to whom you present yourselves slaves to obey, you are that one's slaves whom you obey, whether of sin leading to death, or of obedience leading to righteousness?" (Romans 6:16).

A person becomes a sinner when he submits to "the lust of the flesh, the lust of the eyes, and the pride of life" (1 John 2:16).

Babies are not born with sin. Jesus confirmed this when he said: "Let the little children come to Me, and do not forbid them; for of such is the kingdom of God" (Luke 18:16).

QUESTION #5:

Who is a sinner?

Biblical Response:

"[F]or all have sinned and fall short of the glory of God" (Romans 3:23).

"All we like sheep have gone astray; We have turned, every one, to his own way; And the LORD has laid on Him [Jesus] the iniquity of us all" (Isaiah 53:6).

"There is none who understands; There is none who seeks after God. They have all turned aside; They have together become unprofitable; There is none who does good, no, not one" (Romans 3:11-12).

QUESTION #6:

Are all humans subject to sinning?

Biblical Response:

"If we say that we have no sin, we deceive ourselves, and the truth is not in us" (1 John 1:8).

The apostle Paul said: "For I know that in me (that is, in my flesh) nothing good dwells" (Romans 7:18). "[P]ut off, concerning your former conduct, the old man which grows corrupt according to the deceitful lusts" (Ephesians 4:22).

Comment:

The "old man" is the natural man, who is inclined to sin. All of us, therefore, are sinners and, as such, are held accountable before God. All sinners are in need of God's forgiveness.

QUESTION #7:

What are the results of sin?

Biblical Response:

"And you He made alive, who were dead in trespasses and sins" (Ephesians 2:1).

"For the wages of sin is death, but the gift of God is eternal life in Christ Jesus our Lord" (Romans 6:23).

"Therefore I said to you that you will die in your sins; for if you do not believe that I am He, you will die in your sins" (John 8:24).

QUESTION #8:

What is the remedy for our sins?

Biblical Response:

Jesus said: "I am the way, the truth, and the life. No one comes to the Father except through Me" (John 14:6).

"Much more then, having now been justified by His blood, we shall be saved from wrath through Him" (Romans 5:9).

"In Him [Jesus] we have redemption through His blood, the forgiveness of sins, according to the riches of His grace" (Ephesians 1:7).

Comment:

Without accepting Jesus as the Lord of one's life and without being washed in the blood of Christ (immersed in the waters of baptism), a sinner is still separated from God and is in danger of His wrath.

QUESTION #9:

What does it mean to repent?

Biblical Response:

"For godly sorrow produces repentance leading to salvation, not to be regretted" (2 Corinthians 7:10).

"The Lord is not slack concerning His promise, as some count slackness, but is longsuffering toward us, not willing that any should perish but that all should come to repentance" (2 Peter 3:9).

"[Y]our iniquities have separated you from your God; And your sins have hidden His face from you" (Isaiah 59:2).

Comment:

Repentance is defined as a "feeling of sorrow ... especially for wrongdoing; ... remorse" (*Webster's* 1215). Biblical repentance requires a change of mind as to the course one is following and the adoption of a remorseful attitude in one's heart.

Repentance begins when we come to see sin as God sees sin. When we see the filth and ugliness of sin and the effect it has on our lives, we will then have godly sorrow, which leads to repentance (2 Corinthians 7:9).

QUESTION #10:

What are the three motives God uses in bringing a sinner to repentance?

Comment:

1. God wants us to be aware of the coming judgment. "Truly, these times of ignorance God overlooked, but now commands all men everywhere to repent, because He has appointed a day on which He will judge the world in righteousness by the Man [Jesus] whom He has ordained. He has given assurance of this to all by raising Him [Jesus] from the dead" (Acts 17:30-31).

2. God wants mankind to be aware of His goodness. "[D]o you despise the riches of His goodness, forbearance, and longsuffering, not knowing that the goodness of God leads you to repentance? But in accordance with your hardness and your impenitent heart you are treasuring up for yourself wrath in the day of wrath and revelation of the righteous judgment of God" (Romans 2:4-6).

3. God has given each of us a free will. With our free will we make the decision to hear and heed God's Word. If any person chooses to reject God's invitation to repent, that individual is rejecting God.

VIII.

GRACE

Grace is a gift from God freely given out of the generosity of His heart. This gift of grace cannot be earned nor can it be deserved. Grace is God's redemption at Christ's expense.

QUESTION #1:
When does a person receive grace?

Catholic Response:
"The principal ways of obtaining grace are prayer and the sacraments, especially the Holy Eucharist" (*Baltimore Catechism* 62).

Biblical Response:
"For by grace you have been saved through faith, and that not of yourselves; it is the gift of God, not of works, lest anyone should boast" (Ephesians 2:8-9).

"Even so then, at this present time there is a remnant according to the election of grace. And if by grace, then it is no longer of works; otherwise grace is no longer grace. But if it is of works, it is no longer grace; otherwise work is no longer work" (Romans 11:5-6).

QUESTION #2:

By what means do we receive grace?

Catholic Response:

"Grace is a supernatural gift of God bestowed on us through the merits of Jesus Christ for our salvation. ... There are two kinds of grace: sanctifying grace and actual grace. ... Sanctifying grace is that grace which confers on our souls a new life, ... Actual grace is a supernatural help of God which enlightens our mind and strengthens our will to do good and to avoid evil" (*Baltimore Catechism* 60-61).

Biblical Response:

"For if by one man's offense death reigned through the one, much more those who receive abundance of grace and of the gift of righteousness will reign in life through the One, Jesus Christ" (Romans 5:17).

"But we see Jesus, who was made a little lower than the angels, for the suffering of death crowned with glory and honor, that He, by the grace of God, might taste death for everyone" (Hebrews 2:9).

"Blessed be the God and Father of our Lord Jesus Christ, who has blessed us ... having predestined us to adoption as sons by Jesus Christ to Himself ... to the praise of the glory of His grace, by which He made us accepted in the Beloved. In Him we have redemption through His blood, the forgiveness of sins, according to the riches of His grace" (Ephesians 1:3-7).

"But God demonstrates His own love toward us, in that while we were still sinners, Christ died for us" (Romans 5:8).

QUESTION #3:

What are the blessings of God's grace?

Biblical Response:

Men receive grace from God, who gives us "every spiritual blessing" (Ephesians 1:3). These consist of salvation (Titus 2:11), redemption (Ephesians 1:7), justification (Romans 5:18), peace (Romans 5:1) and a heavenly inheritance" (1 Peter 1:4).

"But by the grace of God, I am what I am, and His grace toward me was not in vain; but I labored more abundantly than they all, yet not I, but the grace of God which was with me" (1 Corinthians 15:10).

QUESTION #4:

Can we receive God's grace in any other way (i.e., through participation in the sacraments designated by the Catholic Church)?

Biblical Response:

"I marvel that you are turning away so soon from Him who called you in the grace of Christ, to a different gospel, which is not another; but there are some who trouble you and want to pervert the gospel of Christ. But even if we, or an angel from heaven, preach any other gospel to you than what we have preached to you, let him be accursed" (Galatians 1:6-8).

QUESTION #5:

How does grace affect our relationship with God?

Biblical Response:

"Now all things are of God, who has reconciled us to Himself through Jesus Christ, and has given us the ministry of reconciliation, that is, that God was in Christ reconciling the world to Himself, not imputing their trespasses to them, and has committed to us the word of reconciliation" (2 Corinthians 5:18-19).

QUESTION #6:

What does the grace of God teach us?

Biblical Response:

"For the grace of God that brings salvation has appeared to all men, teaching us that, denying ungodliness and worldly lusts, we should live soberly, righteously, and godly in the present age" (Titus 2:11-12).

Comment:

The importance of grace is illustrated in the beautiful word-pictures the Bible uses to describe our salvation by the grace of God.

1. By grace we are reconciled with God. "God was in Christ reconciling the world to Himself" (2 Corinthians 5:19). "[W]hen we were enemies we were reconciled to God through the death of His Son" (Romans 5:10).

2. By grace we have been turned away from the wrath of God. "God set forth [Jesus] as a propitiation by His blood" (Romans 3:25).

3. By grace we are adopted by God. "[W]e are no longer under a tutor. For you are all sons of God through faith in Christ Jesus" (Galatians 3:25-26).

4. By grace we receive redemption. "[T]he Son of Man did not come to be served, but to serve, and to give His life a ransom for many" (Matthew 20:28).

5. By grace we are justified by God. "[T]he wages of sin is death" (Romans 6:23), but we are now "being justified freely by His grace through the redemption that is in Christ Jesus" (3:24).

6. By grace we receive forgiveness from God. Peter said, "Repent, and let every one of you be baptized in the name of Jesus Christ for the remission of sins; and you shall receive the gift of the Holy Spirit" (Acts 2:38).

7. By grace we are regenerated. "Therefore, if anyone is in Christ, he is a new creation; old things have passed away; behold, all things have become new" (2 Corinthians 5:17).

IX

AUTHORITY

QUESTION #1:

From whom does all authority come?

Catholic Response:

All Catholic teaching regarding authority in the Catholic Church centers on the Bible, tradition and the magisterium (the authority of the church known as the Apostolic College) (John H. Armstrong 113-114).

Biblical Response:

"All authority has been given to Me in heaven and on earth. Go therefore and make disciples of all the nations, baptizing them in the name of the Father and of the Son and of the Holy Spirit, teaching them to observe all things that I have commanded you; and lo, I am with you always, even to the end of the age" (Matthew 28:18-20).

Hundreds of years before Christ was born, the prophet Isaiah prophesied: "Therefore thus says the Lord GOD: 'Behold I lay in Zion a stone for a foundation, A tried stone, a precious cornerstone, a sure foundation; Whoever believes will not act hastily' " (Isaiah 28:16).

QUESTION #2:

Did Christ give the apostle Peter the authority to govern His church?

Biblical Response:

1. The apostle Peter made this statement of confession to Christ when he was asked who Christ was: "You are the Christ, the Son of the living God" (Matthew 16:16). Jesus said: "And I also say to you that you are Peter, and on this rock I will build My church, and the gates of Hades shall not prevail against it" (v. 18).

2. The apostle Paul also answered this question: "And He [God] put all things under His [Jesus'] feet, and gave Him to be head over all things to the church, which is His body, the fullness of Him who fills all in all" (Ephesians 1:22-23). "He [Jesus] is before all things, and in Him all things consist. And He is the head of the body, the church, who is the beginning, the firstborn from the dead, that in all things He may have the preeminence" (Colossians 1:17-18).

Comment:

The"rock" that Christ referred to with Peter was *"petros,"* a masculine term in Greek meaning a small pebble or a stone detached from a larger rock. The feminine term for the word "rock" is *"petra,"* meaning a ledge or a cliff or a large boulder. This *"petra"* was the rock upon which the church was to be built. If Christ meant to state that the church would be built on Peter, He would have stated it very emphatically. Paul wrote, "For no other foundation can anyone lay than that which is laid, which is Jesus Christ" (1 Corinthians 3:11). "[A]nd all drank the same spiritual drink. For they drank of that spiritual Rock that followed them, and that Rock was Christ" (10:4).

Christ is the builder of His church; the foundation is the rock of truth that Jesus is the Christ, the Son of God. Peter's faith in Christ identified Jesus as a rock. The ecclesiastical supremacy of Peter is nowhere affirmed by Christ, claimed by Peter or acknowledged by the rest of the apostles.

QUESTION #3:

Who is the foundation of the church?

Biblical Response

"For no other foundation can anyone lay than that which is laid, which is Jesus Christ" (1 Corinthians 3:11).

QUESTION #4:

Was Peter the first pope?

Biblical Response:

Consider the following:

1. If Peter is the church's foundation, the church is no longer spiritual, for it was built on a man.
2. Peter denied Christ three times (Matthew 26:69-75) – even cursing and swearing (v. 74).
3. Is the Catholic Church built on a man who had to be rebuked by the apostle Paul for acting like a hypocrite (cf. Galatians 2:14)?
4. The apostle Peter was a married man. He had a wife and a mother-in-law (Matthew 8:14).
5. Peter never allowed himself to be called reverend, father or pope. He referred to himself as a "fellow elder" (1 Peter 5:1). Jesus said, "Do not call anyone on earth your father; for One is your Father, He who is in heaven" (Matthew 23:9). Peter would not accept personal worship from men.
6. Peter taught that we should speak "as the oracles of God" (1 Peter 4:11).
7. Peter exalted Christ as the chief cornerstone (1 Peter 2:4-8).
8. The other apostles never recognized Peter as having more authority than they.
9. The early church did not address Peter with titles of honor or supremacy.
10. Peter called himself "an apostle," one among several (1 Peter 1:1).

QUESTION # 5:

What did Jesus teach about the exercising authority?

Biblical Response:

"You know that the rulers of the Gentiles lord it over them, and those who are great exercise authority over them. Yet it shall not be so among you; but whoever desires to become great among you, let him be your servant" (Matthew 20:25-26).

QUESTION #6:

Can the Roman Catholic Church claim "apostolic succession"?

Biblical Response:

The word "apostle" refers to "one sent." Jesus was the first "Apostle and High Priest" (Hebrews 3:1). Christ was sent from heaven by His Father. The apostles were sometimes referred to as messengers; they were to reveal the plan of salvation to mankind.

Jesus called, trained and sent this group of men (apostles) as His ambassadors and eyewitnesses. Peter was one of these who filled this office. No one can possibly be a successor other than these individuals. No living man can meet the qualifications to be an apostle today, which include the following:

1. An apostle had to be an eyewitness to Jesus. See the process for filling the place of Judas (Acts 1:21-22). The apostle Paul was a special apostle to the Gentiles, and He did see Jesus (1 Corinthians 9:1).

2. An apostle had to have miraculous powers and could impart these powers to others (Acts 2:4, 6; 2 Corinthians 12:12).

3. An apostle had to "be baptized with the Holy Spirit" (Acts 1:5).

4. The other apostles were equally inspired to bind and loose. This authority, given by Christ, was granted to all of the apostles (Matthew 16:19).

X.

THE CHURCH

QUESTION #1:
When did the church begin?

Biblical Response:

The church was established in Jerusalem on the first Pentecost after Jesus' resurrection (about A.D. 30). The Holy Spirit was sent to His apostles, enabling them to proclaim powerfully the gospel (Acts 2:1-4). "[T]he Lord added to the church daily those who were being saved" (v. 47).

QUESTION #2:
Who established the church?

Biblical Response:

Christ established the church when He said: "[O]n this rock I will build My church" (Matthew 16:18). Jesus gave Himself for the church. His own blood became the purchase price for the church (Acts 20:28).

QUESTION # 3:

How is the church identified?

Biblical Response:

The church is pictured as a body, the body of Christ (Ephesians 1:22-23). Christ is the head of the body (Colossians 1:18). The church is also pictured as a kingdom, the kingdom of heaven (Matthew 16:18-19). The church is subject to the authority of Christ. The church is also pictured as a bride, the bride of Christ (Romans 7:4). The church is God's dwelling place and God's habitation.

QUESTION #4:

How many churches did Christ establish?

Biblical Response:

"There is one body and one Spirit, just as you were called in one hope of your calling; one Lord, one faith, one baptism; one God and Father of all, who is above all, and through all, and in you all" (Ephesians 4:4-6).

"Nor is there salvation in any other, for there is no other name under heaven given among men by which we must be saved" (Acts 4:12).

QUESTION #5:

What denomination names are not found in God's Word?

Comment:

1. The Roman Catholic Church was founded in 606 when Boniface II declared himself as the first bishop (Jennings 9).
2. The Lutheran Church was founded in 1517 by Martin Luther in Germany (Jennings 23).
3. The English Episcopal Church was founded during 1531–1539 by Henry VIII in England (Jennings 35).
4. The Presbyterian Church was founded in the 1530s by John Calvin in Switzerland (Jennings 29).
5. The Baptist Church was founded in 1607 by John Smyth in Holland (Jennings 51).
6. The Methodist Church was founded in 1729 by John Wesley in England (Jennings 43).

7. The Mormon Church of Jesus Christ of Latter-day Saints was founded in 1830 by Joseph Smith in Fayette, N.Y. (Jennings 75).

8. The Seventh Day Adventist Church was founded in 1843 by William Miller in New York (Jennings 67).

9. The Christian Scientist Church was founded in 1866 by Mary Baker Eddy in Portland, Maine (Jennings 99).

10. The Jehovah's Witness Church was founded in 1872 by Charles T. Russell in Pittsburgh, Pa. (Jennings 91).

11. The Pentecostal Church was founded in 1899 by groups of denominational people in Topeka, Kan. (Jennings 107).

More than 1,000 other denominations have been founded by men and women over a period of 2,000 years after the Lord's church began on the Day of Pentecost (Tucker 4-13).

QUESTION #6:

Is one church as good as another?

Biblical Response:

"I am the vine, you are the branches. He who abides in Me, and I in him, bears much fruit; for without Me you can do nothing. If anyone does not abide in Me, he is cast out as a branch and is withered; and they gather them and throw them into the fire, and they are burned. If you abide in Me, and My words abide in you, you will ask what you desire, and it shall be done for you" (John 15:5-7).

"Whoever transgresses and does not abide in the doctrine of Christ does not have God. He who abides in the doctrine of Christ has both the Father and the Son" (2 John 1:9).

Comment:

The Lord did not establish different churches with conflicting creeds, doctrines and forms of worship. Nor did He intend that His followers join different denominations. In 1 John we read of the warning given to those seeking to worship God: "Beloved, do not believe every spirit, but test the spirits, whether they are of God; because many false prophets have gone out into the world" (1 John 4:1).

QUESTION #7:

What are the names of Christ's church found in the New Testament?

Comment:

1. church(es) of God	Acts 20:28; 1 Corinthians 1:2; 11:16
2. church of the firstborn	Hebrews 12:23
3. churches of Christ	Romans 16:16
4. bride of Christ	2 Corinthians 11:2
5. house of God; church of the living God	1 Timothy 3:15
6. the church	Matthew 16:18; Acts 2:47
7. kingdom of the Son	Colossians 1:13

(Each name refers to God or Christ and not to any man.)

QUESTION #8:

Of what does the New Testament church consist?

Biblical Response:

The members of the New Testament Church are a part of a called-out body of people over whom Christ reigns as head and in whom the Holy Spirit dwells (Ephesians 1:22; Colossians 1:18).

The New Testament church is known for its simplicity and the beauty of its organization.

QUESTION #9:

How is the Lord's church organized?

Comment:

The church that Jesus established is self-governing, consisting of independent assemblies. Each congregation is autonomous, having no central headquarters linking churches together. The Lord's church is not governed by councils, synods, general assemblies, conferences or any other human organization. It is not a denomination. The church is under the supreme head of Christ, who has absolute divine authority. The inspired apostle Paul declared that God gave Christ to be "head over all things to the church, which is His body" (Ephesians 1:22-23).

QUESTION #10:

How is the leadership of the New Testament church organized?

Biblical Response:

1. Christ delegated authority to elders (also called bishops, overseers, pastors and shepherds). Each congregation selects and appoints its elders. They are Christ's administrators, operating under the Bible and the lordship of Christ. In Titus, the Holy Spirit directed the apostle Paul concerning elders: "appoint elders in every city as I commanded you – if a man is blameless, the husband of one wife, having faithful children not accused of dissipation or insubordination. For a bishop must be blameless, as a steward of God, not self-willed, not quick-tempered, not given to wine, not violent, not greedy for money, but hospitable, a lover of what is good, sober-minded, just, holy, self-controlled, holding fast the faithful word as he has been taught, that he may be able, by sound doctrine, both to exhort and convict those who contradict" (Titus 1:5-9; see also 1 Timothy 3:1-7).

   The apostle Paul spoke to the elders at Ephesus saying: "[T]ake heed to yourselves and to all the flock, among which the Holy Spirit has made you overseers, to shepherd the church of God which He purchased with His own blood" (Acts 20:28).

2. Deacons are also special servants in the local congregation who are appointed by the elders and serve under their direction. "Likewise deacons must be reverent, not double-tongued, not given to much wine, not greedy for money, holding the mystery of the faith with a pure conscience. But let these also first be tested; then let them serve as deacons, being found blameless" (1 Timothy 3:8-10).

3. In the New Testament church, men serve as preachers, evangelists or ministers. They are not known as "reverend" as this term is used only one time in the Bible (King James Version) and refers only to God: "He [God] sent redemption unto his people: he hath commanded his covenant for ever: holy and reverend is his name" (Psalm 111:9).

   The preacher is hired by the elders to preach the gospel. "How then shall they call on Him in whom they have not believed? And

how shall they believe in Him of whom they have not heard? And
how shall they hear without a preacher?" (Romans 10:14).
4. Members are the church, the body of Christ. They are called by
several names, including believers (Acts 5:14), saints (Acts 9:13;
Romans 1:7), priests (1 Peter 2:5, 9), sons of God (Galatians
3:26), and Christians (Acts 11:26). The members participate in
the worship service, fellowship with other Christians, give fi-
nancially (as they have been prospered) to meet the needs of
the congregation, and use their talents to follow Christ's Great
Commission (Matthew 28:18-20) by spreading the gospel to the
unsaved throughout the world.

QUESTION #11:

Can a person be saved and go to heaven without belonging to a New
Testament church?

Biblical Response:

The apostle Paul was "not ashamed of the gospel of Christ, for it is the
power of God to salvation for everyone who believes" (Romans 1:16).

God wants us to study and learn His Word. He will not accept igno-
rance as an excuse on the day of judgment. "[T]hese times of ignorance
God overlooked, but now commands all men everywhere to repent"
(Acts 17:30).

The doctrines of men are not the teachings that lead to salvation.
This is confirmed in the book of Romans: "[I]n the day when God
will judge the secrets of men by Jesus Christ, according to my gospel"
(Romans 2:16).

In 2 Thessalonians, we learn the importance of obeying the truth of
God's revealed and inspired Word: "The coming of the lawless one
is according to the working of Satan, with all power, signs, and lying
wonders, and with all unrighteous deception among those who perish,
because they did not receive the love of the truth, that they might be
saved. And for this reason God will send them strong delusion, that
they should believe the lie" (2 Thessalonians 2:9-11).

QUESTION #12:

What spiritual acts of worship are specified in the New Testament church?

Biblical Response:

God has given a pattern of worship for His church in the New Testament just as surely as He gave a pattern of worship for the Israelites in the Old Testament. Jesus told a Samaritan woman He met at a well that "God is Spirit, and those who worship Him must worship in spirit and truth" (John 4:24).

The church of the New Testament has five acts of worship that are scriptural and follow the pattern Christ established for His church:

1. Singing: "[S]peaking to one another in psalms and hymns and spiritual songs" (Ephesians 5:19).

2. Giving: "Now concerning the collection for the saints, as I have given orders to the churches of Galatia, so you must do also: On the first day of the week let each one of you lay something aside, storing up as he may prosper, that there be no collections when I come" (1 Corinthians 16:1-2).

3. Praying: "I desire that the men pray everywhere, lifting up holy hands, without wrath and doubting" (1 Timothy 2:8).

4. Bible Teaching: "[T]hose who gladly received his word were baptized; and that day about three thousand souls were added to them. And they continued steadfastly in the apostles' doctrine and fellowship, in the breading of bread, and in prayers" (Acts 2:41-42).

5. Partaking of the Lord's Supper: "[O]n the first day of the week [Sunday], when the disciples came together to break bread, Paul, ready to depart the next day, spoke to them and continued his message until midnight" (Acts 20:7).

Comment:

When the Christians assembled to break bread on Sunday, they remembered the death, burial and resurrection of Jesus. This remembrance consisted of each person eating unleavened bread and drinking the fruit of the vine in memory of Christ who gave His body and shed His blood so that mankind would be redeemed.

QUESTION #13:

What is of primary importance in the work of the New Testament church?

Biblical Response:

"How beautiful are the feet of those who preach the gospel of peace" (Romans 10:15).

"[W]e are ambassadors for Christ, as though God were pleading through us: we implore you on Christ's behalf, be reconciled to God" (2 Corinthians 5:20).

A letter from the apostle Paul to Timothy encouraged him with these words: "And the things that you have heard from me among many witnesses, commit these to faithful men who will be able to teach others also" (2 Timothy 2:2).

The true church of the New Testament is committed to doing mission work and taking the gospel to the ends of the earth. This ministry is for both men and women.

QUESTION #14:

What other works are of vital importance to the church of the New Testament?

Comment:

1. A further work of the church is to help the needy, an act known as benevolence. The church puts into practice the teaching of Jesus by caring for widows, orphans and others in need. All Christians are to help and give of their talents as each opportunity presents itself to saints and sinners alike (Romans 12:13-18).

2. A secondary work of the church is to help its members grow in the knowledge of the gospel through biblical studies and various activities for different age groups within the body.

3. Fellowship is of vital importance for both the spiritual and physical needs of its members.

QUESTION #15:

What terms of membership are necessary to be added to the church of the New Testament?

Biblical Response:

Requirements for church membership and salvation consist of the following:

1. Hearing the gospel: "So then faith comes by hearing, and hearing by the word of God" (Romans 10:17).
2. Believing the gospel: "But without faith it is impossible to please Him, for he who comes to God must believe that He is, and that He is a rewarder of those who diligently seek Him" (Hebrews 11:6).
3. Repenting of present and past sins: "Repent therefore and be converted, that your sins may be blotted out, so that times of refreshing may come from the presence of the Lord" (Acts 3:19).
4. Confessing Christ as the Son of God: "Then Philip said: 'If you believe with all your heart, you may [be baptized].' And he answered and said, 'I believe that Jesus Christ is the Son of God'" (Acts 8:37).
5. Being baptized into Christ for the remission of your sins: "Repent, and let every one of you be baptized in the name of Jesus Christ for the remission of sins; and you shall receive the gift of the Holy Spirit" (Acts 2:38). "He who believes and is baptized will be saved; but he who does not believe will be condemned" (Mark 16:16). "There is also an antitype which now saves us – baptism (not the removal of the filth of the flesh, but the answer of a good conscience toward God), through the resurrection of Jesus Christ" (1 Peter 3:21). "For as many of you as were baptized into Christ have put on Christ" (Galatians 3:27).
6. Remaining faithful until death: "[A]s newborn babes, desire the pure milk of the word, that you may grow thereby" (1 Peter 2:2).

TRADITION AND TRUTH

PART A

THE SEVEN RITES (SACRAMENTS) OF THE ROMAN CATHOLIC CHURCH

QUESTION:
What is a sacrament?

Catholic Doctrine:

Sacraments are used in the worship of the Roman Catholic Church as sacred rites using signs and gestures. These visible signs and gestures communicate God's invisible grace and love to the recipient. In other words, "[a] sacrament is an outward sign instituted by Christ to give grace" (*Baltimore Catechism* 144).

"Jesus has given His church the sacraments as the very sources of His presence within her. The sacraments sustain and give life to the Catholic Church, and she builds her whole existence around them: they are the air she breathes, and the food she eats" (Chilson 129).

"There are seven sacraments: Baptism, Confirmation, Holy Eucharist, Penance, Anointing of the Sick, Holy Orders, and Matrimony" (*Baltimore Catechism* 145). Each of these sacraments will be addressed individually and examined biblically in this chapter.

Biblical Response:

The system of the sacraments is not taught in the New Testament. "It is the Spirit who gives life; the flesh profits nothing. The words that I speak to you are spirit, and they are life" (John 6:63).

Comment:

We partake of Christ by coming to Him and believing in Him. Jesus said: "I am the bread of life. He who comes to Me shall never hunger, and he who believes in Me shall never thirst" (John 6:35).

Any material, physical thing (notably, the sacraments) cannot give the spiritual life of God's grace. Jesus laid down this biblical principle in John 6:63.

The Roman Catholic Church cannot designate the conditions by which one receives God's grace. The grace that is given by God came through His righteousness and is in the mind of God. The apostle Paul stated how this biblical principle is lived out: "For we are the circumcision, who worship God in the Spirit, rejoice in Christ Jesus, and have no confidence in the flesh" (Philippians 3:3).

God's grace is given to us as a gift, not because of our works or by our participation in the sacraments as designated by the Roman Catholic Church. Once again, Paul explained: "For by grace you have been saved through faith, and that not of yourselves; it is the gift of God, not of works, lest anyone should boast" (Ephesians 2:8-9). "[S]o that as sin reigned in death, even so grace might reign through righteousness to eternal life through Jesus Christ our Lord" (Romans 5:21).

God's grace is received by baptized believers who have obeyed the gospel, have come to Jesus in faith and believe in His promises. The sacramental system of Catholicism has no biblical authority, nor is it ordained or approved by God's Holy Spirit.

SACRAMENT #1

Baptism

QUESTION #1:

What is the sacrament of Baptism?

Catholic Doctrine:

"In the first century all Christian converts were baptized as adults. A problem then arose as to whether the children should be baptized immediately or should they grow up and request baptism. The community decided that their children should be baptized. Because they were born into a Christian home and their parents would raise them in the faith, the children did not have to make a decision for their faith as an adult could. So the body of Christ now included children who could grow up physically and spiritually in the body of the Catholic Church. As Europe became Christian, soon most baptisms were of children. It remains so today" (Chilson 131).

"Children should be baptized as soon as possible after birth" (*Baltimore Catechism* 154). The Roman Catholic Church teaches that a baby is born with the stain of original sin on his soul. It teaches that this sin is inherited from Adam. For the soul to become "born again" and cleansed, the sacrament of Baptism must be administered. A priest pours water upon the baby's forehead, blessing the child in the name of the Father, Son and the Holy Spirit. Through this process, all sins are forgiven; the child's name is entered into the community of the church, and he becomes a child of God, bonded forever to the Lord (151-156).

Biblical Response:

"[U]nless you are converted and become as little children, you will by no means enter the kingdom of heaven" (Matthew 18:3).

"You were perfect in your ways from the day you were created, Till iniquity [sin] was found in you" (Ezekiel 28:15).

"Truly, this only I have found: That God made man upright, But they have sought out many schemes" (Ecclesiastes 7:29).

Comment:

Babies are not born with the guilt of sin, for "sin is lawlessness" (1 John 3:4). Jesus held babies as the example of purity and humility. Therefore, they do not need to be baptized. God's Word addresses the actual event when sin occurs within one's life: "But each one is tempted when he is drawn away by his own desires and enticed. Then, when desire has conceived, it gives birth to sin; and sin, when it is full-grown, brings forth death" (James 1:14-15). In this passage, death refers to the death of the soul. Babies are not tempted to sin, nor do they choose to sin. Sin occurs at the age when one can reason.

QUESTION #2:

Why is baptism necessary for salvation?

Biblical Response:

"He who believes and is baptized will be saved; but he who does not believe will be condemned" (Mark 16:16).

QUESTION #3:

How many baptisms are there?

Catholic Doctrine:

There are three kinds of baptism: Baptism of water, Baptism of blood and Baptism of desire. "[O]nly Baptism of water actually makes a person a member of the Church. ... Baptism of blood or desire makes a person a member of the Church in desire. These are the two lifelines trailing from the sides of the Church to save those who are outside the Church through no fault of their own. ... An unbaptized person receives the baptism of blood when he suffers martyrdom for the faith of Christ. ... An unbaptized person receives the baptism of desire when he loves God above all things and desires to do all that is necessary for his salvation" (*Baltimore Catechism* 153-154).

Biblical Response:

There is "one Lord, one faith, one baptism; one God and Father of all, who is above all, and through all, and in you all" (Ephesians 4:5-6).

Comment:

Those baptized according to the New Testament are those who have reached the age of accountability. They are first taught, and only those capable of hearing the Word of God, believing it, repenting of their sins and confessing Jesus as Lord are immersed for the remission of their sins. If a person believes that Jesus Christ is the Son of God and desires to be saved, he needs to be baptized. Jesus Himself placed baptism between belief and salvation.

These effects occur when one is baptized according to God's revealed and inspired Word:

1. Salvation: "He who believes and is baptized will be saved; but he who does not believe will be condemned" (Mark 16:16).

2. Remission of sins: "Then Peter said to them, 'Repent and let every one of you be baptized in the name of Jesus Christ for the remission of sins; and you shall receive the gift of the Holy Spirit'" (Acts 2:38).

3. Unity with Christ: "[D]o you not know that as many of us as were baptized into Christ Jesus were baptized into His death? Therefore we were buried with Him through baptism into death, that just as Christ was raised from the dead by the glory of the Father, even so we also should walk in newness of life. For if we have been united together in the likeness of His death, certainly we also shall be in the likeness of His resurrection" (Romans 6:3-5). "For as many of you as were baptized into Christ have put on Christ" (Galatians 3:27).

Baptism is "the answer of a good conscience toward God" (1 Peter 3:21). Once a person is baptized, he is added to the kingdom of God (Acts 2:41, 47). The names are then "written in the Lamb's Book of Life" (Revelation 21:27).

All church historians agree that immersion occurred in the first-century church. It was changed to pouring or sprinkling in the sixth century. Jesus gave the command to all of His disciples before leaving this earth to preach the gospel and to baptize: "All authority has been given to Me in heaven and on earth. Go therefore and make disciples of all the nations, baptizing them in the name of the Father and of the Son and of the Holy Spirit, teaching them to observe all things that I have commanded you; and lo, I am with you always, even to the end of the age" (Matthew 28:18-20).

If the Bible teaches that accountable individuals must be baptized to be saved and if a person has not been baptized, his eternal destination is in jeopardy. The Greek word for baptism is *"baptizo,"* which means "to immerse." The Bible teaches that when a person is immersed in the blood of Christ through water baptism, he obtains pardon for all his past sins. If a person is not immersed before death, he will remain lost forever. However, God is the final judge of each individual. Obedience to the gospel's teaching on water baptism is the most important decision each of us must make this side of heaven.

SACRAMENT #2
Confirmation

QUESTION:
What is the sacrament of Confirmation, and is it taught in the Bible?

Catholic Doctrine:

"Confirmation is the sacrament through which the Holy Spirit comes to us in a special way and enables us to profess our faith as strong and perfect Christians and soldiers of Jesus Christ" (*Baltimore Catechism* 157).

"The Roman Catholic Church teaches that the sacrament of Confirmation perfects baptismal grace. In this sacrament the baptized person is given the Holy Spirit to strengthen his or her faith when one is confirmed by the local bishop. The one being confirmed also receives the gifts of wisdom, understanding, counsel, fortitude and fear of the Lord" (*Baltimore Catechism* 157-161).

Biblical Response:

Jesus promised the Holy Spirit to the apostles in a special dispensation for these purposes:

1. To bring to the apostles' memory things Jesus had taught them during His public ministry, guiding them into all truth and showing them the things that were to come. "He who does not love Me does not keep My words; and the word which you hear is not Mine but the Father's who sent Me" (John 14:24).

2. To enable the apostles to lay hands on others who would help to strengthen the church spiritually and to edify the body of Christ as a whole (1 Corinthians 12:1-11; Ephesians 4:11-14).

The gift of the Holy Spirit was also promised to all who are obedient children of God and obey the gospel. "And we are His witnesses to these things, and so also is the Holy Spirit whom God has given to those who obey Him" (Acts 5:32).

Comment:

Not one word of Scripture upholds the doctrine for the sacrament of Confirmation. Not one instance in the New Testament justifies giving this sacrament to any individual for the purpose claimed by the hierarchy in Rome. The sacrament of Confirmation is a man-made doctrine adopted and instituted by the Roman Catholic Church in A.D. 1215 and still upheld as a biblical doctrine today. (See Section 1:III for other questions referring to the work of the Holy Spirit.)

SACRAMENT #3
Holy Eucharist

QUESTION #1:

What is the sacrament of the Holy Eucharist or the doctrine of the "Real Presence"?

Catholic Doctrine:

The sacrament of the Holy Eucharist (or the doctrine of the "Real Presence") teaches that the wafer used during the Mass becomes the actual body and blood of Christ, although Christ remains under the appearances of bread and wine. The Holy Eucharist is considered the greatest of all the sacraments because the bread and the wine are converted into the real presence of Jesus during the consecration at Mass. This process is considered a mystery and is known as "transubstantiation." This belief stems from the Roman Catholic Church's interpretation of John 6:54-55 (*Baltimore Catechism* 162-167).

Biblical Response:

"I am the living bread which came down from heaven. If anyone eats of this bread, he will live forever; and the bread that I shall give is My flesh, which I shall give for the life of the world" (John 6:51). "Most assuredly, I say to you, unless you eat the flesh of the Son of Man and drink His blood, you have no life in you. Whoever eats My flesh and drinks My blood has eternal life, and I will raise him up at the last day. For My flesh is food indeed, and My blood is drink indeed. He that eats My flesh and drinks My blood abides in Me, and I in him" (vv. 53-56).

"When Jesus knew in Himself that His disciples complained about this, He said to them, 'Does this offend you? What then if you should see the Son of Man ascend where He was before? It is the Spirit who gives life; the flesh profits nothing. The words that I speak to you are spirit, and they are life'" (John 6:61-63).

Comment:

Jesus gives the true meaning of His words at the Last Supper (John 6:53-55). He wanted them to understand the meaning of eating His flesh and drinking His blood in a human manner. Therefore, He used the bread and the wine to have His disciples remember Him through these elements He had chosen. Jesus wanted them to never forget that He is the "bread of life" (v. 48), and He is also the "living water" (John 4:10-14) because of which they would never thirst. Jesus had no intention of returning to earth through the process of transubstantiation.

"The word transubstantiation comes from the Latin '*trans*' (beyond) and '*substantia*' (substance). This was defined by the Lateran Council of A.D. 1215 which stated the following: 'the wonderful and singular conversion of the whole substance of the wine into the Blood of Christ and the bread into the Body of Christ and the species of bread and wine alone remaining'" (Sparagna 172-74).

Jesus knew what He was about to suffer, and He wanted His disciples to look forward to His Second Coming. He was preparing them for the time when they would receive the Holy Spirit. We receive the Holy Spirit not by eating a piece of flesh but by hearing God's Word, believing it and obeying it through baptism. The apostle Paul's letter to the Corinthians refers to the instructions given to him personally by Jesus. These instructions were to clarify the concept of eating His flesh and drinking His blood. Jesus wanted all Christians to show reverence and honor in their remembrance of the Lord's Last Supper: "'Take, eat; this is My body which is broken for you; do this in remembrance of Me.' In the same manner He also took the cup after supper, saying, 'This cup is the new covenant in My blood. This do, as often as you drink it, in remembrance of Me.' For as often as you eat this bread and drink this cup, you proclaim the Lord's death till He comes" (1 Corinthians 11:24-26).

QUESTION #2:

Is the sacrament of the Holy Eucharist taught in the Bible?

Biblical Response:

"It is the Spirit who gives life; the flesh profits nothing. The words that I speak to you are spirit, and they are life" (John 6:63).

Comment:

Jesus Christ did not institute the Catholic Mass. The Mass developed through a gradual evolution and transformation of the Lord's Last Supper. Jesus did not envision the Mass or something like it to become the central act of worship, expressed through the idea of transubstantiation. But Jesus did command participation in the Lord's Supper upon the first day of every week.

SACRAMENT #4
Penance

QUESTION #1:
What is the sacrament of Penance?

Catholic Doctrine:

"Penance is the sacrament by which sins committed after Baptism are forgiven through the absolution of the priest. ... Only God can forgive sins. But He can decide for Himself how He wants to do it. And the way He has decided upon is to use priests as His instruments" (*Baltimore Catechism* 184-185).

Through the sacrament of Penance, the priest, in the place of Christ, absolves a penitent's sin once he makes a statement of contrition and says a penance required by the priest hearing the confession. The penitent is then absolved of any sins he has committed after baptism. Because of his forgiveness, he receives "the restoration or increase of sanctifying grace" for his soul (*Baltimore Catechism* 185).

Biblical Response:

"If we confess our sins, He is faithful and just to forgive us our sins and to cleanse us from all unrighteousness" (1 John 1:9).

"There is therefore now no condemnation to those who are in Christ Jesus" (Romans 8:1).

"Nor is there salvation in any other, for there is no other name under heaven given among men by which we must be saved" (Acts 4:12).

"[I]f anyone sins, we have an Advocate with the Father, Jesus Christ the righteous. And He Himself is the propitiation for our sins, and not for ours only but also for the whole world" (1 John 2:1-2).

"Let the wicked forsake his way, And the unrighteous man his thoughts; Let him return to the LORD, And He will have mercy on him; And to our God, For He will abundantly pardon" (Isaiah 55:7).

Comment:

God's Word provides the answer for salvation from past sins. The time when one is pardoned comes through his or her obedience to God's Word.

Jesus said, "Not every one who says to Me, 'Lord, Lord,' shall enter the kingdom of heaven, but he who does the will of My Father in heaven" (Matthew 7:21).

"He became the author of eternal salvation to all who obey Him" (Hebrews 5:9).

Repentance and obedience are the key factors for forgiveness. When one is a baptized believer, he can have an assurance of salvation without depending upon a priest for absolution. We can take God at His word when He says: "For by grace you have been saved through faith, and that not of yourselves; it is the gift of God, not of works, lest anyone should boast" (Ephesians 2:8-9).

QUESTION #2:

Does any man have the authority to forgive sins?

Catholic Response:

"The priest has the power to forgive sins from Jesus Christ, who said to His apostles and to their successors in the priesthood: 'Receive the Holy Spirit; whose sins you shall forgive, they are forgiven them; and whose sins you shall retain, they are retained'" (*Baltimore Catechism* 185).

Biblical Response:

"[W]hatever you bind on earth will be bound in heaven, and whatever you loose on earth will be loosed in heaven" (Matthew 16:19).

"[T]hrough this Man is preached to you the forgiveness of sins" (Acts 13:38).

"Confess your trespasses to one another, and pray for one another, that you may be healed" (James 5:16).

Comment:

The power to forgive sins was not exercised on Pentecost nor at any other time by any of the apostles. They never acted as officials of the church to forgive others of their sins. When the apostles were given the keys to the kingdom of heaven, they opened the treasures of the gospel. Whatever the gospel bound, they bound, and whatever it loosed, they loosed. Those who obeyed the gospel were forgiven of their sins. Those who did not obey remained bound in their sins. A baptized believer is given the ministry of reconciliation (2 Corinthians 5:17-19).

QUESTION #3:
What is meant by the royal priesthood?

Biblical Response:

Every Christian is a priest as identified in the following scripture: "But you are a chosen generation, a royal priesthood, a holy nation, His own special people, that you may proclaim the praises of Him who called you out of darkness into His marvelous light; who once were not a people but are now the people of God, who had not obtained mercy but now have obtained mercy" (1 Peter 2:9-10).

Comment:

Under the Old Covenant in the Old Testament, certain qualifications made an individual acceptable as a priest before God. He had to come from the tribe of Levi. If those seeking to be priests were not found in the genealogy, they were excluded and considered defiled (Ezra 2:62). This covenant was characterized by a kingdom of priests.

Under the New Covenant in the New Testament, Christians are identified as baptized believers and are God's priests. The sacrifice a Christian makes to God is a living one: "I beseech you therefore, brethren, by the mercies of God, that you present your bodies a living sacrifice, holy, acceptable to God, which is your reasonable service" (Romans 12:1).

It is important that we, as God's priests, "continually offer the sacrifice of praise to God" (Hebrews 13:15). Our priestly offerings should also include our effort to do good and to communicate the Word of God to those seeking truth. As part of the royal priesthood, we are to intercede to God for others and be available to those in need. Every Christian is a minister, one of God's servants. We are to declare the excellencies of Christ to a world that lies in darkness. As one of God's priests, we

must be fired up by our faith in Christ and have a passion for souls
to herald His good news wherever we go. No greater honor has been
bestowed on those who are part of the royal priesthood.

SACRAMENT #5
Anointing of the Sick

QUESTION:
Is the sacrament of the Anointing of the Sick recognized by the Scriptures?

Catholic Doctrine:
In the Old Testament, sickness was experienced as a sign of weakness
and bound up with sin. The prophets encouraged the sick to live in the
presence of God from whom the people implored healing. In the Roman
Catholic Church today, a sacrament has been instituted especially for
those who need healing. This is called the sacrament of the Anointing
of the Sick. Anyone who is a faithful member of the Roman Catholic
Church can receive this sacrament. It is administered by a priest. The sick
one is anointed with oil blessed by the bishop. This anointing takes place
on the forehead and on the hands of the sick person. The church teaches
that the sick person receives a special grace that gives them comfort,
peace, courage and even the forgiveness of their sins. "A special part
of the anointing is the receiving of 'Viaticum,' (Holy Eucharist), which
helps the person leave this life as they go into eternity" (Ratzinger 92;
see also *Baltimore Catechism* 209-211).

Biblical Teaching:
"Is anyone among you sick? Let him call for the elders of the church,
and let them pray over him, anointing him with oil in the name of the
Lord. And the prayer of faith will save the sick, and the Lord will raise him
up. And if he has committed sins, he will be forgiven" (James 5:14-15).

Comment:
God's plan of pardon for the child of God who sins is that he repent,
confess his sins to God and ask His forgiveness. The one sick has
no assurance that he will be forgiven because of his participation in
the sacrament of the Anointing. The Catholic priest has no scriptural

authority to forgive sins or administer any special rites to the dying. The Lord often used symbols when He healed the sick. The oil required in this text was probably olive oil, which is still very therapeutic and used symbolically. This was to be done in the name of the Lord. It is up to the Lord whether the sick person becomes healed.

SACRAMENT #6
Holy Orders

QUESTION:

Does the sacrament of Holy Orders ordain a man as a priest in the sight of God?

Catholic Response:

The sacrament of Holy Orders is how one becomes part of the priesthood in the Roman Catholic Church. A specially appointed group of men claim the exclusive right to perform the Sacrifice of the Mass and to forgive sins committed against God. This claim rests on the idea that the apostles had men who would be their successors and that their authority was passed on to those successors today. A priest is ordained as a mediator. He then becomes a mediator between God and man, whose work is to unite man with God (*Baltimore Catechism* 211-215).

Biblical Response:

To be a successor of the apostles, the Bible identifies six qualifications required for men proclaiming succession today.

1. They must have seen Jesus personally: "[Y]ou will be His witness to all men of what you have seen and heard" (Acts 22:15).

2. They had the power to speak in a language they had not been taught: " And they [the apostles] were all filled with the Holy Spirit and began to speak with other tongues, as the Spirit gave them utterance" (Acts 2:4).

3. They had the power to work many kinds of miracles: "Truly the signs of an apostle were accomplished among you with all perseverance, in signs and wonders and mighty deeds" (2 Corinthians 12:12).

4. They had the power to confer the Holy Spirit upon others (Acts 8:14-17).

5. They received the Holy Spirit to remember everything Jesus had taught: "But the Helper, the Holy Spirit, whom the Father will send in My name, He will teach you all things, and bring to your remembrance all things that I said to you" (John 14:26).

6. They received the Spirit of truth and were guided into all truth: "[W]hen He, the Spirit of truth, has come, He will guide you into all truth; for He will not speak on His own authority, but whatever He hears He will speak; and He will tell you things to come" (John 16:13).

SACRAMENT #7
Matrimony

QUESTION:

Does God recognize the sacrament of Matrimony also called the sacrament of Marriage or the sacrament of Life-Giving Oneness?

Catholic Doctrine:

Christ raised matrimony to the dignity of a sacrament. This sacrament is to be used as a symbol of God's faithfulness and His unconditional love. A marriage is celebrated at a Mass with the presence of a priest and several witnesses. A "mixed" marriage occurs between a Catholic and a non-Catholic. This marriage must be approved with the permission of the "ecclesiastical authority." The couple must agree to raise their children in the Roman Catholic doctrine. Marriage, as a sacrament, bestows upon the spouses the grace necessary to attain holiness in their married life and to accept with responsibility the gift of children and to provide for their education.

"The sins of adultery, polygamy and homosexuality are opposed to this sacrament. When the spouses separate, remarry or enter into a 'same-sex' marriage, they cannot take communion or receive sacramental absolution" (Ratzinger 98).

Biblical Response:

The Bible does not refer to marriage as a sacrament. These words in Ephesians express this union between a man and a woman: " 'For this reason a man shall leave his father and mother and be joined to his wife, and the two shall become one flesh.' This is a great mystery, but

I speak concerning Christ and the church. Nevertheless let each one of you in particular so love his own wife as himself, and let the wife see that she respects her husband" (5:31-33).

The apostle Paul laid the firm foundation for a solid and secure marriage in Ephesians 5:22-33: "Wives, submit to our own husbands, as to the Lord. For the husband is head of the wife, as also Christ is head of the church; and He is the Savior of the body."

Comment:

Divorce produces many of the dilemmas and tragedies of our time. It is a breakdown of the institution God created. It is a violation of a vow taken before God by both parties. God takes these vows seriously and so must the couple who makes them. The seriousness of divorce in God's sight is stated in the following scripture: "Furthermore it has been said, 'Whoever divorces his wife, let him give her a certificate of divorce.' But I say to you that whoever divorces his wife for any reason except sexual immorality causes her to commit adultery; and whoever marries a woman who is divorced commits adultery" (Matthew 5:31-32).

Christ did not give any church the authority to annul a marriage. The only time remarriage is acceptable in the sight of the Lord is when one of the mates dies or when a marriage is dissolved because of adultery. The word "remarriage" is not identified in the Word of God. God is not against marriage, but He is against breaking the marriage vow and sinning against it.

In the book of John, we read of Jesus meeting a woman caught in the act of adultery and about to be stoned by her accusers. Jesus words were very significant. "[Jesus] said to her, 'Woman, where are those accusers of yours? Has no one condemned you?' She said, 'No one, Lord.' And Jesus said to her, 'Neither do I condemn you; go, and sin no more'" (John 8:10-11). God wants those in marriage to consider all the consequences of divorce. Sin, even the sin of divorce, has consequences.

THE SACRIFICE OF THE MASS

QUESTION #1:

How is the Holy Eucharist related to the Sacrifice of the Mass?

Catholic Doctrine:

"The Mass is the sacrifice of the New Law in which Christ, through the ministry of the priest, offers Himself to God in an unbloody manner under the appearances of bread and wine" (*Baltimore Catechism* 168).

Catholicism teaches that the Holy Eucharist is not only a sacrament but a "sacrifice" as well. This sacrifice is accomplished in the Mass, one of the most sublime acts of worship that is given to Catholics by our Lord. But the Mass is not a mere representation of the cross. It is a continuation of the sacrifice that Jesus gave on the cross. This shedding of His blood is done "mystically." The Roman Catholic Church teaches that this is the sacrifice Christ requested His followers do until the end of time (*Baltimore Catechism* 168-176).

Biblical Response:

" … not that He [Christ] should offer Himself often, as the high priest enters the Most Holy Place every year with blood of another – He then would have had to suffer often since the foundation of the world; but now, once at the end of the ages, He has appeared to put away sin by the sacrifice of Himself" (Hebrews 9:25-26).

"Christ was offered once to bear the sins of many" (Hebrews 9:28). "For by one offering He has perfected forever those who are being sanctified" (10:14).

Comment:

Each of us must understand the powerful meaning of the sacrifice Christ made for us. Through Christ's sacrifice, peace has been restored between God and mankind. Through Christ's sacrifice, Satan is overcome, and we have been set free from his tyrannies. Through Christ's sacrifice, we have the forgiveness of our sins, and eternal life is given to all who put their faith and obedience in Him. Through Christ's sacrifice, we have the liberty to enter the "Holy of Holies" of God's presence and present ourselves before His throne with our cares, our petitions and our love for Him and His precious Son. Jesus is now our brother and advocate before the throne of God. "He is the Mediator of the new covenant, ... that those who are called may receive the promise of the eternal inheritance" (Hebrews 9:15).

The New Testament makes it very clear that no one needs to repeat any sacrifice for our sins. In Acts and in the epistles, we read of God's recommendation for our need to pray, give praise, grow in God's grace, have a contrite spirit, and preach the gospel to the lost. Nothing is stated in God's Word about participating in the Sacrifice of the Mass as instituted by the Roman Catholic Church.

QUESTION #2:

How often should the Holy Eucharist be received?

Catholic Response:

"It is well to receive Holy Communion often, even daily, because this intimate union with Jesus Christ, the Source of all holiness and the Giver of all graces, is the greatest aid to a holy life" (*Baltimore Catechism* 181).

Biblical Response:

The correct terminology is the Lord's Supper or communion, and the observance of this should be every Sunday (Acts 20:7).

PART C

VENERATION OF MARY

QUESTION #1:

Is the veneration of Mary honored in the Scriptures?

Catholic Doctrine:

"In an encyclical entitled *Redemptoris Mater*, Pope John Paul II wrote: 'The Virgin Mary is not only the mother of Jesus, but she is also the Mother of God. Like her Son, Jesus, she was conceived as a human being, exempt from any trace of original sin.' In 1854, a papal bull entitled *Ineffabilis Deus* was declared by Pope Pius IX. This dogma stated Mary had been conceived without sin. It also stated she remained free from personal sin during her lifetime here on earth. Before, during, and after the birth of her son, Mary remained physically a virgin, and at her death, she was taken up – body and soul into heaven. Because of her position as the mother of Jesus, she was not allowed to see death. We honor her assumption on a special day known as the Assumption. This dogma was proclaimed in 1950. The Catholic Church, taught by the Holy Spirit, reverences her with filial affection and devotion. Because of her motherly love, she cares for her Son's sisters and brothers, who still journey on earth. She is, in the words of Vatican II, the sign of certain hope and comfort to all in need" (Schrotenboer 37-41).

Biblical Response:

... to Mary's sinlessness: Mary referred to God as her Savior (Luke 1:47). She was not above being human nor is she to be honored as deity. Mary was a sinner. God alone is holy (Luke 18:19; Revelation 15:4). God did not create a being equal to Himself. "As it is written: 'There is none righteous, no, not one'" (Romans 3:10). "[F]or all have sinned and fall short of the glory of God" (v. 23). "But the Scripture has confined all under sin, that the promise by faith in Jesus Christ might be given to those who believe" (Galatians 3:22).

... to the Immaculate Conception of Mary: The doctrine that Mary, the mother of Jesus, was conceived without sin is unscriptural. Mary's mother was a sinner when she conceived Mary. Likewise, Mary was a sinner when she conceived Jesus. God's Word establishes the fact that we are all sinners: "If we say that we have no sin, we deceive ourselves, and the truth is not in us" (1 John 1:8). "If we say that we have not sinned, we make Him a liar, and His word is not in us" (v. 10).

The Catholic Church verifies the doctrine of the Immaculate Conception by using the salutation given by the angel Gabriel to Mary: "Rejoice highly favored one, the Lord is with you; blessed are you among women!" (Luke 1:28). This Scripture says nothing about Mary being free from sin. The apostle Paul affirmed this without any exception: "[F]or all have sinned and fall short of the glory of God, being justified freely by His grace through the redemption that is in Christ Jesus" (Romans 3:23-24). The apostle Paul further emphasized the universality of sin held by all mankind in Romans: "Therefore, just as through one man sin entered the world, and death through sin, and thus death spread to all men, [including Mary] because all sinned" (Romans 5:12). Moreover, the psalmist David described the corruption of the natural man: "There is none who does good, No, not one" (Psalm 14:3).

Sin is not something inherited; rather, one chooses to commit sin. "The soul who sins shall die" (Ezekiel 18:4, 20). "[E]ach one is tempted when he is drawn away by his own desires and enticed. Then, when desire has conceived, it gives birth to sin; and sin, when it is full grown, brings forth death" (James 1:14-15). "And as it is appointed for men to die once, but after this the judgment" (Hebrews 9:27).

... **to Mary's perpetual virginity:** The Bible clearly teaches that Mary became the wife of Joseph (Matthew 1:16, 20; Luke 2:41) and that Jesus had four brothers and some sisters. "Then Joseph ... took to him his wife, and did not know her till she had brought forth her first-born Son" (Matthew 1:24-25). "[W]hat wisdom is this which is given to Him, that such mighty works are performed by His hands! Is this not the carpenter, the son of Mary, and brother of James, Joses, Judas, and Simon? And are not His sisters here with us?" (Mark 6:2-3). "While He was still talking to the multitudes, behold, His mother and brothers stood outside, seeking to speak with Him. Then one said to Him, 'Look, Your mother and Your brothers are standing outside, seeking to speak with You'" (Matthew 12:46-47).

The apostle John distinguished the term "brothers" from His disciples by saying: "After this He [Jesus] went down to Capernaum, He, His mother, His brothers, and His disciples" (John 2:12). Jesus stated His position on how He felt about His family saying: "Who is My mother and who are My brothers?" (Matthew 12:48). [W]hoever does the will of My Father in heaven is My brother and sister and other" (v. 50). "And it happened, as He spoke these things, that a certain woman from the crowd raised her voice and said to Him, 'Blessed is the womb that bore You, and the breasts which nursed You!' But He said, 'More than that, blessed are those who hear the word of God and keep it!'" (Luke 11:27-28).

... **to the bodily assumption of Mary:** In Ecclesiastes we read: "Then the dust will return to the earth as it was, And the spirit will return to God who gave it" (Ecclesiastes 12:7). Mary, like every other human being who has died, awaits the final judgment. Death is the penalty for sin. There is no scriptural proof or evidence that Mary has been taken bodily into heaven.

... **to Mary as a mediator and an advocate between God and man:** The apostle Paul stated: "For there is one God and one Mediator between God and men, the Man Christ Jesus, who gave Himself a ransom for all, to be testified in due time" (1 Timothy 2:5-6).

Comment:

The above teachings and dogmas regarding Mary, the mother of Jesus

Christ, are contrary to the Scriptures of the New Testament. Everything the Bible states about Mary is true. She was a blessed and important person (Luke 1:28-35), and she was specially chosen by God's Holy Spirit to conceive her Son, Jesus, miraculously. Mary was a descendant of David and a devout Jewess. She remained faithful to her husband Joseph and gave him other sons and daughters. No doubt, Jesus obeyed His mother as a child and honored her as His earthly mother in His manhood. Her outstanding qualities as a mother and wife are humility, obedience and submission to the will of God.

However, neither God, Jesus nor any of the apostles gave Mary any special recognition or authority to use divine power on earth or in heaven. The dogmas, miracles and apparitions along with her ability to be the mediator between God and man cannot be found anywhere in Scripture. The Bible clearly identifies the person we are to petition with our requests.

QUESTION #2:

Is it biblical to pray to Mary through the rosary?

Catholic Doctrine:

Praying the rosary is a means of salvation because a true child of Mary is never lost and one who says the rosary daily is truly Mary's child. A prayer to Mary found on a holy card distributed by the International Fatima Rosary Crusade states the following: "O God of infinite goodness and mercy, fill our hearts with a great confidence in our Most Holy Mother Mary, whom we invoke under the title of the Immaculate Heart of Mercy, and grant us by her most powerful intercession, all the graces, spiritual and temporal, which we need through Christ our Lord. Amen."

Biblical Response:

"Most assuredly, I say to you, whatever you ask the Father in My name He will give to you ... In that day you will ask in My name, and I do not say to you that I shall pray the Father for you; for the Father Himself loves you, because you have loved Me, and have believed that I came forth from God" (John 16:23, 26-27). Mary herself rejoiced in God as her Savior. "My soul magnifies the Lord, And my spirit has rejoiced in God my Savior" (Luke 1:46-47). Christ clearly stated: "Why do you call Me good? No one is good but One, that is, God" (Mark 10:18).

Comment:

The Bible never addresses or even hints that Mary is an essential mediator through whom salvation and all grace flow. Nowhere in Scripture are we taught to entrust our wants through Mary's intervention. As stated in the above Scriptures, God's Word is very clear that we come to the Father through Jesus Christ alone. If Mary were alive today, she would rebuke all false doctrines, prayers and various intercessions made in her name. Mary, like the rest of humanity, was considered a sinner. The Word of God affirms this in Romans 3:23: "for all have sinned and fall short of the glory of God."

CANONIZATION OF THE SAINTS AND VENERATION OF RELICS

QUESTION:

Does the Bible honor the canonization of individuals to sainthood? Does the Bible authorize the veneration of relics of those individuals proclaimed saints by the Roman Catholic Church?

Catholic Doctrine:

The Catholic Church teaches that individuals can petition the saints by offering up their prayers through the saints, thereby making intercession to God and obtaining benefits from God through His Son Jesus (Council of Trent).

Biblical Response:

The Scriptures repudiate all worship to dead people considered to be saints because Christ is the only Savior, only Mediator and only way to God.

Old Testament: The following scriptures in the Old Testament oppose veneration of relics, graven images and invocations to the proclaimed saints sanctified by the Roman Catholic Church. In Deuteronomy, we learn how God felt about worship through images. His warning came through the Ten Commandments, which He gave to Moses on Mount Sinai: "You shall have no other gods before Me. You shall not make for yourself a carved image – any likeness of anything that is in heaven above, or that is in the earth beneath, or that is in the water under the earth; you shall not bow down to them nor serve them. For I, the LORD your God, am a jealous God, visiting the iniquity of the fathers upon the children to the third and fourth generations of those who hate Me." (Deuteronomy 5:7-9).

In Numbers 21:9, we read where God told Moses to make a bronze serpent. Those who were bitten by a serpent should look at it. Once they did, they were healed. King Hezekiah later broke the image of the snake because the people had begun to burn incense before it (2 Kings 18:4). Other cases of honoring images are condemned in Leviticus 26:1, Isaiah 40:18 and Jeremiah 44:3. In Exodus 20:4-5, God is very clear about whom we should worship: "You shall not make for yourself a carved image – any likeness of anything that is in heaven above, or that is in the earth beneath, or that is in the water under the earth; you shall not bow down to them nor serve them" (Exodus 20:4-5). Another look at the Old Testament reveals God's condemnation of idol worship: "Give no regard to mediums and familiar spirits; do not seek after them, to be defiled by them: I am the LORD your God" (Leviticus 19:31).

New Testament: Veneration of images and worshiping saints are also condemned in the New Testament. "Nor is there salvation in any other, for there is no other name under heaven given among men by which we must be saved" (Acts 4:12). Jesus alone is to be worshiped and honored. He says: "I am the way, the truth, and the life. No one comes to the Father except through Me" (John 14:6). "Let us therefore come bodily to the throne of grace, that we may obtain mercy and find grace to help in time of need (Hebrews 4:16). "God is Spirit, and those who worship Him must worship in spirit and truth" (John 4:24).

"[A]s I was passing through and considering the objects of your worship, I even found an altar with this inscription: TO THE UNKNOWN GOD. Therefore, the One whom you worship without knowing, Him I proclaim to you: God, who made the world and everything in it, since He is Lord of heaven and earth, does not dwell in temples made with hands. Nor is He worshiped with men's hands, as though He needed anything, since He gives to all life, breath, and all things. And He has made from one blood every nation of men to dwell on all the face of the earth, and has determined their preappointed times and the boundaries of their dwellings, so that they should seek the Lord, in the hope that they might grope for

Him and find Him, though He is not far from each one of us; for in Him we live and move and have our being" (Acts 17:23-28). In 1 John 5:21, the Bible gives a warning: "Little children, keep yourselves from idols."

Comments:

I thoroughly understand the reasons why people honor and venerate images and relics. When I made my final profession and took my vows of poverty, chastity and obedience as a Roman Catholic nun in 1959, I was given a crucifix. This crucifix was to be worn on my breast as a sign of being a full-fledged professed Sister of St. Joseph. Within my crucifix was placed the bone of a canonized saint. Her name was Saint Maria Goretti. She lived in Italy and died at 13, having been murdered by a neighbor boy.

I treasured that relic. Although I no longer venerate it, I recall the honor and privilege I was given to carry that relic within my crucifix. Over the years, the relic became lost, and the crucifix now lies among a collection of memorabilia I have kept since leaving convent life. Little did I know then, but now I understand the reason why God forbids invocation to the saints, relics or graven images. When Jesus was tempted by Satan, He cautioned him against worshiping idols, images and relics saying: "[I]t is written, 'You shall worship the LORD your God, and Him only you shall serve'" (Luke 4:8).

Although we are no longer under the Law of the Old Testament but under grace, we cannot disregard God's Laws, for we are free only from the penalty of that law (Hebrews 10:1-4).

INDULGENCES

QUESTION:

What are indulgences, and does the Roman Catholic Church have the power and authority to grant indulgences?

Catholic Doctrine:

The Catholic teaching on an indulgence is defined as the taking away of all or part of the temporal punishment because of sin. Even though forgiveness of sins frees us from the penalty of eternal punishment, justice requires some punishment in this life in reparation for our forgiven sins. This is known as "temporal punishment." One can receive a "plenary indulgence" (full remission) or a "partial indulgence" (part remission) of sins. An indulgence is a limited period of release from punishment due to committing sin. Four requirements are necessary to gain an indulgence:

1. Be free from mortal sin and be in the state of grace.

2. Say the prayers or do the work to which the indulgence is attached.

3. Have the intention of gaining the indulgence.

4. Fulfill all conditions required by the Catholic Church (Council of Trent).

"Since the power of granting indulgences was granted by Christ to the Church, and she has, even in most ancient times, used the power of granting indulgences delivered to her, the Holy Synod teaches, that the use of granting indulgences is approved by this sacred council"

(Council of Trent). Matthew 16:19 and Matthew 18:18 were applied to the doctrine of indulgences. Following Vatican II, indulgences are not mentioned in any of the church's updated ecclesiastical literature.

Biblical Response:

"'For My thoughts are not your thoughts, Nor are your ways My ways,' says the LORD. 'For as the heavens are higher than the earth, So are My ways higher than your ways, And My thoughts than your thoughts'" (Isaiah 55:8-9).

"It is not in man who walks to direct his own steps" (Jeremiah 10:23).

"There is a way that seems right to a man, But its end is the way of death" (Proverbs 14:12).

"Not everyone who says to Me, 'Lord, Lord,' shall enter the kingdom of heaven, but he who does the will of My Father in heaven" (Matthew 7:21).

"The Father loves the Son, and has given all things into His hand. He who believes in the Son has everlasting life; and he who does not believe the Son shall not see life, but the wrath of God abides on him" (John 3:35-36).

Comment:

The idea of indulgences does not exist according to the doctrines revealed in God's inspired Word. What is God's will and His remedy for the forgiveness of both the temporal and eternal punishment because of sin? Salvation. The remedy is very simple:

1. Believe and obey God and His truth as presented in His Word.
2. Repent (turn completely away from sin): "Repent therefore and be converted, that your sins may be blotted out, so that times of refreshing may come from the presence of the Lord, and that He may send Jesus Christ" (Acts 3:19-20; see also Acts 17:30-31; Romans 2:4).
3. Confess Jesus alone as the Lord of your life.
4. [B]e baptized [immersed] ... for the remission of sins (Acts 2:38; 1 Peter 3:21). In Mark 16:16 we read: "He who believes and is baptized will be saved; but he who does not believe will be condemned."
5. Remain faithful unto death to the commitment you made at baptism.

PART F

PURGATORY
AND
JUDGMENT

QUESTION #1:

What is purgatory, and can indulgences be applied to this state of existence?

Catholic Doctrine:

"Those are punished for a time in purgatory who die in the state of grace but are guilty of venial sin, or have not fully satisfied for the temporal punishment due to their sins" (*Baltimore Catechism* 90). "In purgatory, God's cleansing fires burn away the soul's selfishness till its love becomes perfect and it is ready to fly to heaven" (91).

The following Scripture is used by Roman Catholicism to justify this state: "If anyone's work which he has built on it endures, he will receive a reward. If anyone's work is burned, he will suffer loss; but he himself will be saved, yet so as through fire" (1 Corinthians 3:14-15).

"Purgatory is a place where a soul is deprived of its heavenly reward and suffers cleansing pain, a purification of fire after death. Some call this process 'purging.' The length of time one remains in this state is unknown. Prayers for the deceased, and merits derived from spiritual works, can be earned by the living and applied to an individual's soul believed to be in Purgatory" (Ryan 109-116). The doctrine of the existence of Purgatory is taken from the book of 2 Maccabees 12:39-45

(Douay Bible). This doctrine is defined as "a place where souls are detained and are helped by the prayers of the faithful and by the Sacrifice of the Mass" (Council of Trent).

Comment:

The books of Maccabees are in the Apocrypha, written after the close of the Old Testament canon and not included in the canon of Scripture. The books of the Apocrypha are of doubtful origin. The passage adopted by the Council of Trent did not address the purging and purification process by fire that a soul experiences in purgatory. In regard to the afterlife and the end times, Paul wrote this to the church at Thessalonica to reassure them: "Now may the God of peace Himself sanctify you completely; and may your whole spirit, soul, and body be preserved blameless at the coming of our Lord Jesus Christ" (1 Thessalonians 5:23).

Biblical Doctrine:

First John teaches that our cleansing and purging from sin are based entirely on the finished work of Christ: "If we confess our sins, He is faithful and just to forgive us our sins, and to cleanse us from all unrighteousness" (1:9).

The book of Isaiah speaks unmistakably about God's gracious pardon to repentant sinners: "Though your sins are like scarlet, They shall be as white as snow; Though they are red like crimson, They shall be as wool" (1:18).

In the book of Micah, we learn of God casting sins and punishment in the bottom of the sea: "You will cast all our sins Into the depths of the sea" (7:19).

Comment:

Neither purgatory nor indulgences are mentioned or even alluded to in the Old or New Testaments. The practice of praying for the souls of the deceased and presenting a place of purification for sinners after death was instituted by Pope Gregory in the sixth century. The teaching of God's grace and the shedding of His blood for the remission of our sins is absent from this false doctrine. The Bible teaches that perfect righteousness is not acquired through any process derived by men, but only through our faith and obedience to Christ (Galatians 2:16).

QUESTION #2:
Where are the dead?

Catholic Doctrine:
There are three places where a soul can be sent after death. The first is heaven, the second is purgatory, and the third is hell. Those who die in mortal sin and choose to live apart from God go to hell, the ungodly place of torment in the next life where the souls of those who are damned suffer forever. They will stay there for all eternity. They will suffer all the pains of hell: darkness, sadness and remorse; and they will live with all those who hate goodness. Pits of fire are in hell, but the greatest pain will be separation from God. "Heaven is the place, or state, of perfect happiness" with God in the next life (*Baltimore Catechism* 92). The souls in heaven know unspeakable happiness. Each soul will receive its own reward according to his labors while on earth (90-92).

Biblical Response:
The apostle Paul taught that our whole nature is body, soul and spirit as stated in 1 Thessalonians 5:23. The body is the flesh, and the soul often refers to the whole man (Acts 2:41). Sometimes the spirit is used interchangeably with the soul. The spirit of a person dwells within the body. "The LORD ... forms the spirit of man within him" (Zechariah 12:1). In Job, we read the following: "But there is a spirit in man, And the breath of the Almighty gives him understanding" (Job 32:8). Man's spirit is immortal, for the spirit of man lives beyond death (1 Corinthians 15:51-54). In Genesis and Ecclesiastes, God told us: "For dust you are, And to dust you shall return" (Genesis 3:19). "Then the dust will return to the earth as it was, And the spirit will return to God who gave it" (Ecclesiastes 12:7).

This truth is further emphasized by Christ on the cross, speaking to a penitent thief. There was no need for any type of repentance after death for the thief. "And Jesus said to him, 'Assuredly, I say to you, today you will be with Me in Paradise'" (Luke 23:43). While on the cross, Jesus spoke of His own spirit saying: "Father, 'into Your hands I commend My spirit'" (v. 46). Second Peter 1:13-15 compares death to putting off the tent or the dwelling place where a person lived while on earth. The spirits of all people live on in eternity. Those who die physically are still living in their spirit, awaiting the day of judgment as recorded in Revelation 6:9-11.

The biblical meaning of death includes three types of death: physical, spiritual and eternal. Physical death is the separation of the soul and body (James 2:26). Spiritual death is separation of the soul from God (Ephesians 2:1). Eternal death is separation from God forever in hell (Matthew 25:46). All humans have eternal existence in one of two states – some in happiness because of an obedient life and others in torment because of their refusal to accept God's commands (Luke 16:19-31). Christ described the afterlife in this account of Lazarus and the rich man. Two facts can be learned from this parable. First, death is not extinction, for the spirit survives the decay of the body and lives after the body has turned to dust. Second, spirits without their bodies are in a state of consciousness, happy or miserable, depending on the choices they made on earth. In this state, they can no longer communicate with this world.

The Bible teaches that man's spirit is capable of a separate and conscious existence when the body is dissolved. The apostle Paul described this conscious existence when he talked about the third heaven (2 Corinthians 12:2-4). "'Eye has not seen, nor ear heard, Nor have entered into the heart of man The things which God has prepared for those who love Him.' But God has revealed them to us through His Spirit. For the Spirit searches all things, yes, the deep things of God" (1 Corinthians 2:9-10).

QUESTION #3:

What happens after death, and when will judgment occur?

Catholic Doctrine:

In the prayer of the Apostles Creed (a statement of Catholic beliefs), the last section contains the following: "I believe … [in] the resurrection of the body, and life everlasting." The Roman Catholic Church teaches there will be a second coming of Christ on the earth at the end of the world. "He will come sitting on the clouds of heaven and His angels with Him. The bodies of all those who have died will rise and go to meet Him" in the air. This is known as the "resurrection of the body." At this time, all men will be reunited with their souls. Immediately after the resurrection of all humans, there will be a general judgment. During this judgment, "the justice, wisdom, and mercy of God may be glorified in the presence of all." This will be a public declaration of the sentences or rewards already given or made in the particular judgment. "The judgment which will be passed on each one of us immediately after death is called the particular judgment" (*Baltimore Catechism* 10, 88-89).

Mary, the mother of Jesus, is the only person that was reunited with her immaculate soul. She was glorified and taken into heaven. This teaching became dogma in 1950.

Biblical Response:

"And as it is appointed for men to die once, but after this the judgment" (Hebrews 9:27).

"For we shall all stand before the judgment seat of Christ" (Romans 14:10). "So then each of us shall give account of himself to God" (v. 12)

At death, the spirit of each individual goes to a place prepared by the Lord called hades. In Luke 16:23, the spirits of both the rich man and Lazarus were in hades. (See Matthew 11:23; Luke 10:15; Acts 2:27, 31). Hades (or the hadean realm) is the unseen or invisible world where all spirits are placed after death. It is divided into two compartments: (1) Paradise – the abode of the righteous; (2) Tartarus – the abode of the wicked. When all are resurrected from their graves and appear at the final judgment (Matthew 25:31-46), each will go to his or her final destination – the saved or righteous to heaven and the unsaved or wicked to Gehenna, the place of hell and fire.

Comment:

Those who believe in purgatory need to understand that after death there is no opportunity for an individual to change his or her life's record. When the spirit of each person enters into the hadean world, its destiny is sealed. A person's life on earth determines his or her place in hades. Likewise the deeds on earth will determine the eternal reward (Romans 14:12; 2 Corinthians 5:10). The Bible says nothing about "probation" after death.

The Bible does not teach that a place called purgatory exists after death. This doctrine was upheld by the Catholic Church in the 11th century and approved by the Council of Trent in 1545–1563. Jesus told of a rich man and a beggar named Lazarus and identified the two places that hold the spirits of the dead. After the personal judgment of each spirit following one's death, they either enter the bosom of Abraham (which is Paradise) or Tartarus (which is a place of torment). A great chasm separates these two places (Luke 16:19-31).

QUESTION #4:

Are Mary, the mother of Jesus, and the canonized saints proclaimed by the Catholic Church in heaven today?

Biblical Response:

"No one has ascended to heaven but He who came down from heaven, that is, the Son of Man" (John 3:13).

Comment:

The spirits in hades or Sheol (the temporary place for the spirits of the dead) will be reunited with their bodies to face the judgment at the white throne of God at the final judgment. They will be evaluated as to whether they accepted Jesus as Lord and Savior, obeyed the gospel and lived faithfully (Revelation 13:8; 20:10-15; 1 Peter 4:17).

The evil ones who rejected the Holy Spirit's teachings, followed their own man-made doctrines and traditions, and were not baptized in the blood of Christ will go to Gehenna (hell) after the final judgment (John 5:28-29). The Bible describes hell several times as a place where "the fire … shall never be quenched – 'Their worm does not die'" (Mark 9:43-44). Hell will be a place of eternal darkness where everything and everyone is separated from God (Matthew 8:12; 22:13; 25:30).

PART G

HEAVEN

QUESTION #1:
Is there a heaven?

Comment:

Many people believe that living a good life and being kind to others is the way to heaven. The Bible teaches only one way to gain entrance into heaven – through a relationship with Jesus Christ (John 14:6). A relationship with God is not based on rituals, sacraments and rules. Instead it is based on grace, forgiveness and a right standing with God through obedience to His revealed and inspired Word (2 Thessalonians 1:7-9). The following Scriptures relate to the wonders of heaven.

Biblical Response:

Old Testament: "I watched till thrones were put in place, And the Ancient of Days was seated; His garment was white as snow, And the hair of His head was like pure wool. His throne was a fiery flame, Its wheels a burning fire; A fiery stream issued And came forth from before Him. A thousand thousands ministered to Him; Ten thousand times ten thousand stood before Him. The court was seated, And the books were opened …

"I was watching in the night visions, And behold, One like the Son of Man, Coming with the clouds of heaven! He came to the Ancient of Days, And they brought Him near before Him. Then to Him was given dominion and glory and a kingdom, That all peoples, nations, and languages should serve Him. His dominion is an everlasting dominion, Which shall not pass away, And His kingdom the one Which shall not be destroyed" (Daniel 7:9-14).

New Testament: "Eye has not seen, nor ear heard, Nor have entered into the heart of man The things which God has prepared for those who love Him" (1 Corinthians 2:9).

"For we know that if our earthly house, this tent, is destroyed, we have a building from God, a house not made with hands, eternal in the heavens" (2 Corinthians 5:1).

"In My Father's house are many mansions; if it were not so, I would have told you. I go to prepare a place for you. And if I go and prepare a place for you, I will come again and receive you to Myself; that where I am, there you may be also" (John 14:2-3).

"For our citizenship is in heaven, from which we also eagerly wait for the Savior, the Lord Jesus Christ, who will transform our lowly body that it may be conformed to His glorious body, according to the working by which He is able even to subdue all things to Himself" (Philippians 3:20-21).

"No one has ascended to heaven but He who came down from heaven, that is, the Son of Man who is in heaven" (John 3:13).

Comment:

Once we develop an eternal perspective about where we will spend eternity, even the greatest problems on earth fade in significance. It will be a great and everlasting spiritual thrill to worship and have fellowship with the one almighty God in heaven. There will be no more death, no more mourning, no more sadness – forever. God has prepared an unimaginable place for those who have been faithful to Him. Our own imagination cannot even begin to comprehend the endless joys of being in heaven.

While we wait to receive our reward, Jesus wants us to "seek first the kingdom of God and His righteousness, and all these things [that will satisfy all your needs] shall be added to you" (Matthew 6:33).

QUESTION #2:

Does the Bible speak of heaven?

Biblical Response:

Heaven is beyond imagining, beyond all description. The prophet Daniel told us what was revealed to him concerning heaven in Daniel 7:13-14.

In Matthew 13:44-46, Jesus taught a parable describing heaven. In this parable, Jesus proclaimed that heaven would be worth trading everything for the opportunity to go there. The joy of the man at his discovery of hidden treasure and of the merchant in finding a pearl of great price is the joy and the eagerness that should describe us as we look forward to the reward in heaven.

Jesus comforted the disciples as He prepared to return to His heavenly home. He reassured them with these words: "In My Father's house are many mansions; if it were not so, I would have told you. I go to prepare a place for you. And if I go and prepare a place for you, I will come again and receive you to Myself; that where I am, there you may be also" (John 14:2-3).

The word "where" refers to a physical location. Although the disciples were not able to visualize the wonder of heaven until they would arrive, later the apostle Paul clarified what had been revealed to him through the Holy Spirit: "[A]s it is written: 'Eye has not seen nor ear heard, Nor have entered into the heart of man The things which God has prepared for those who love Him'" (1 Corinthians 2:9).

QUESTION #3:

What will heaven look like?

Biblical Response:

"[B]ehold, a throne set in heaven, and One sat on the throne. And He who sat there was like a jasper and a sardius stone in appearance; and there was a rainbow around the throne, in appearance like an emerald. Around the throne were twenty-four thrones, and on the thrones I saw twenty-four elders sitting, clothed in white robes; and they had crowns of gold on their heads. And from the throne proceeded lightnings, thunderings, and voices. Seven lamps of fire were burning before the throne, which are the seven Spirits of God. Before the throne there was a sea of glass, like crystal" (Revelation 4:2-6).

Comment:

The Bible speaks of a new heaven and a new earth to come (Revelation 21:1). This new earth will shine in the brilliance of life emanating from God Himself (v. 11). The tree of life first mentioned in Genesis 2:9 will produce fruit 12 times a year, once each month, and its leaves will serve as medicine for the nations (Revelation 22:2). The apostle Peter reaffirmed this new heaven and new earth when he said, concerning Jesus: "whom heaven must receive until the times of restoration of all things, which God has spoken by the mouth of all His holy prophets since the world began" (Acts 3:21). Peter also addressed another promise Christ made regarding the new heaven and the new earth: "Nevertheless we, according to His promise, look for new heavens and a new earth in which righteousness dwells" (2 Peter 3:13).

QUESTION #4:

Who will be able to enter the gates of heaven?

Biblical Response:

"But there shall by no means enter it anything that defiles, or causes an abomination or a lie, but only those who are written in the Lamb's Book of Life" (Revelation 21:27).

"But the cowardly, unbelieving, abominable, murderers, sexually immoral, sorcerers, idolaters, and all liars shall have their part in the lake which burns with fire and brimstone, which is the second death" (Revelation 21:8).

"Nor is there salvation in any other, for there is no other name under heaven given among men by which we must be saved" (Acts 4:12).

The apostle Paul spoke of a new life in Christ with these words: "[D]o you not know that as many of us as were baptized into Christ Jesus were baptized into His death? Therefore we were buried with Him through baptism into death, that just as Christ was raised from the dead by the glory of the Father, even so we also should walk in newness of life. For if we have been united together in the likeness of His death, certainly we also shall be in the likeness of His resurrection" (Romans 6:3-5).

Jesus told us that refusing to receive His words is rejecting Him: "And if anyone hears My words and does not believe, I do not judge him; for I did not come to judge the world but to save the world. He who rejects Me, and does not receive My words, has that which judges him – the word that I have spoken will judge him in the last day" (John 12:47-48).

Comment:

A Pharisee named Nicodemus, a rabbi and a member of the supreme court of the Jews, came to Jesus at night, questioning Him about His ability to do miraculous things as a man of God. Jesus responded to his questions, saying: " 'I say to you, unless one is born again, he cannot see the kingdom of God.' Nicodemus said to Him, 'How can a man be born when he is old? Can he enter a second time into his mother's womb and be born?' Jesus answered, 'Most assuredly, I say to you, unless one is born of water and the Spirit, he cannot enter the kingdom of God. That which is born of the flesh is flesh, and that which is born of the Spirit is spirit. Do not marvel that I said to you, "You must be born again" ' " (John 3:3-7).

The two elements of "water" and "the Spirit" are essential to the new birth, and the new birth is essential to entering the kingdom of heaven. Only those who have been born again (immersed in water) will have their names written in the Lamb's Book of Life.

QUESTION #5:

What will the saved experience in heaven?

Biblical Response:

"You will show me the path of life; In Your presence is fullness of joy; At Your right hand are pleasures forevermore" (Psalm 16:11).

"Behold, the tabernacle of God is with men, and He will dwell with them, and they shall be His people. God Himself will be with them and be their God" (Revelation 21:3).

"Oh, the depth of the riches both of the wisdom and knowledge of God! How unsearchable are His judgments and His ways past finding out!" (Romans 11:33).

Comment:

Death is something that awaits every human being. Each of us will have to make this journey from which there is no return. God's Word has given us specific information about eternity and the choice each must make in this life prior to the departure for eternity. Our choice will determine where we will spend eternity.

The pathway to heaven is free. It takes a commitment to reject a prideful, self-centered view of life and allow ourselves to be shown the love of God.

By trusting and obeying God's Word and believing in His promises, we can have a relationship with God. He loves each of us deeply and hungers for us to have a relationship with Him.

Because of God's unconditional love, He gave the world the most amazing gift anyone could imagine – the humiliating, painful sacrifice of His only beloved Son so that humanity could be forgiven. When Jesus died on the cross, He said, "It is finished!" (John 19:30). This same statement was written at the top of Greek certificates of debt when they were paid in full. Christ died so that the debt of all our sins could be paid in full. No amount of money, works, novenas, special prayers to individuals already deceased, or any physical sacrifice we make can pay our way into heaven. Jesus paid with His life for us. Because of Jesus' atonement for our sins, God offers each of us forgiveness. Jesus said, "No one comes to the Father except through Me" (John 14:6). Salvation is found in no name other than the name of Jesus (Acts 4:12). Not accepting God's gift of love and forgiveness through His Son Jesus and the prompting of the Holy Spirit will lead to eternal separation from God.

My question to each of the readers of this section on heaven is are you prepared to take this final journey, knowing what you now know about eternity?

CONCLUSION

The completion of *Biblical Answers to Catholic Questions* has been a tremendous learning process for me as the writer. Its contents should lead the reader to explore and discover godly truths Catholicism has neglected to teach. This book is intended to accomplish a very specific biblical goal using a simplified method in presenting godly truths through a question-and-answer format. This approach has allowed me to compare doctrines taught in Roman Catholicism with what is taught in the revealed and inspired Word of God.

In my evaluation of Roman Catholicism through various literary and personal contacts, I have endeavored to present accurately the doctrines, beliefs and practices initially established by the Council of Trent in 1546 and reaffirmed by the Second Vatican Council in 1962. Momentous changes have occurred in the Roman Catholic Church since the commencing of Vatican II. However, these changes have been merely cosmetic. Vatican II has not discarded Catholicism's unscriptural teachings and traditions. Rather, the change has been in the way doctrines are now taught and communicated to parishioners and converts to this man-made institution.

Too many conflicts remain between the accepted traditions and doctrines of the Roman Catholic Church and the Word of God. Most people today no longer understand the teachings in Scripture alone. We live in an age of personality and individuality. How easily we solve the problems of the heart with quick answers received from the advice of human authorities.

My task to measure biblical knowledge against traditional teachings of Roman Catholicism was gargantuan in scope because I also sought the meaning of life and the truth outside of God's revealed and inspired Word. Once my knowledge was awakened to the fallible teachings, unbiblical doctrines and ostentatious rituals of this man-made institution, my view of God and His direction for my life began to change as I searched for His truth. I agreed to seek it in God's Word. As a sincere inquirer, I was open to seek spiritual help from the Bible alone.

In my search for godly truth I began learning a new view of God – what was important to Him and how His teachings could influence every part of my life today and my eternal destiny. One of the first Scriptures I learned and memorized when studying the Word of God is found in 2 Timothy: "All Scripture is given by inspiration of God, and is profitable for doctrine, for reproof, for correction, for instruction in righteousness, that the man of God may be complete, thoroughly equipped for every good work" (3:16-17).

Because of my obedience to accepting God's Word, today I have an inner peace that surpasses all human understanding. Only by God's grace and the power of His Word living in my life will I remain faithful to Him until the day He calls me home. I agree with Paul when he encouraged all of us to "[b]e diligent to present yourself approved to God, a worker who does not need to be ashamed, rightly dividing the word of truth" (2 Timothy 2:15).

Jesus focused His teaching on the kingdom of God. His requirement for entrance into this kingdom demanded obedience to His Father's commands. In Jesus, we find the path to salvation. Jesus expressed it most perfectly when He said: "Most assuredly, I say to you, unless one is born of water and the Spirit, he cannot enter the kingdom of God. That which is born of the flesh is flesh, and that which is born of the Spirit is spirit. Do not marvel that I said to you, 'You must be born again'" (John 3:5-7).

As a former Roman Catholic nun, I learned to love Jesus, but I knew very little about His Father. Jesus became the bridge between the emotional experience I had in my relationship with Him as His bride for 19 years in convent life. Today, I now know and understand that the church is His bride and that Jesus is the Word of God made flesh so that each of us may behold the glory of God His Father. Jesus is the only One who can deliver us from the darkness of limited human knowledge and understanding. He is the only One who can lead us to the light of God's perfect teachings through the instruction of His Holy Spirit.

The search for faith is important to each one who has chosen to seek Jesus, God and the truth delivered by the Holy Spirit in His Word. Your knowledge and inner peace will come to full enlightenment when you know, understand and accept godly truth. The quest for God's truth and inner peace needs to be discovered by your sincere response to the following questions:

1. How do I discover God and His will for my life?
2. What can help me in my search for God?
3. What does God ask of me?
4. What would Jesus have me do?
5. Can I be assured of enjoying eternal happiness with God?

A search for the meaning of life is found in Jesus' life, teachings, death and resurrection. When you reach your destination beyond the veil of this life, only then will you learn whether your choice and acceptance of God's requirements (as revealed by Jesus and His Holy Spirit) were necessary to enter His kingdom. The following Scripture is a strong recommendation from Jesus Himself:

"And if anyone hears My words and does not believe, I do not judge him; for I did not come to judge the world but to save the world. He who rejects Me, and does not receive My words, has that which judges him – the word that I have spoken will judge him in the last day. For I have not spoken on My own authority; but the Father who sent Me gave Me a command, what I should say and what I should speak. And I know that His command is everlasting life. Therefore, whatever I speak, just as the Father has told Me, so I speak" (John 12:47-50).

WORKS CONSULTED AND CITED

Armstrong, J.N. *Undenominational Christianity*. Searcy: Resource, 2002.

Armstrong, John, ed. *Roman Catholicism: Evangelical Protestants Analyze What Divides and Unites Us*. Chicago: Moody, 1994.

Armstrong, John H. *The Catholic Mystery: Understanding the Beliefs and Practices of Modern Catholicism*. Eugene: Harvest House, 1999.

Bausch, William J. *While You Were Gone: A Handbook for Returning Catholics, and Those Thinking About It*. New London: Twenty-Third, 1994.

Boettner, Loraine. *Roman Catholicism*. Philadelphia: Presbyterian & Reformed, 1962.

Chilson, Richard. *An Introduction to the Faith of Catholics*. Mahwah: Paulist Press, 1972.

Cizik, Richard. *The High Cost of Indifference: Can Christians Afford Not to Act?* Norwood: Regal, 1984.

Cogan, William J. *A Brief Catechism for Adults: A Complete Handbook on How to be a Good Catholic*. Charlotte: TAN Books, 2009.

Council of Trent, Session 25. *Canonization and Veneration to the Saints; Declaration of Indulgences*.

Cruden, Alexander. *Cruden's Concordance*. Peabody: Hendrickson, 1872.

DeSiano, Frank P. *Presenting the Catholic Faith: A Modern Catechism for Inquirers*. Mahwah: Paulist Press, 1987.

Dogmatic Constitution on Divine Revelation: Dei Verbum: Solemnly Promulgated by his Holiness Pope Paul VI on November 18, 1965. Documents of Vatican II. Boston: St. Paul Books, 1965.

The Holy Bible: Douay-Rheims Version. Trans. of Latin Vulgate, 1914.

Hunt, Dave. *A Woman Rides the Beast: The Roman Catholic Church and the Last Days*. Eugene: Harvest House, 1994.

Jennings, Alvin. *Traditions of Men Versus the Word of God*. Fort Worth: Star Bible, 2010.

Keating, Karl. *Catholicism and Fundamentalism: The Attack on "Romanism" by "Bible Christians."* San Francisco: Ignatius Press, 1988.

Kelley, Bennet. *The New Saint Joseph Baltimore Catechism*. Rev. ed. New York: Catholic Book Publishing, 1969-1962.

Kersten, John C. *A Short Bible Catechism*. New York: Catholic Book Publishing, 1984.

Kohmescher, Matthew G. *Catholicism Today: A Survey of Catholic Belief and Practice*. New York: Paulist Press, 1980.

Layton, Mac. *The Holy Spirit: A 13 Lesson Study Course*. Edmond: Christian Publishing Co., 1966.

Lightfoot, Neil R. *How We Got the Bible*. Grand Rapids: Baker, 1993.

Lockyer, Herbert. *All the Doctrines of the Bible*. Grand Rapids: Zondervan, 1964.

Matthews, Paul. *Basic Errors of Catholicism*. Murfreesboro: DeHoff Publications, 1965.

Nevins, Albert J. *Answering a Fundamentalist*. Huntington: Our Sunday Visitor Publishers, 2006.

Ratzinger, Cardinal Joseph and Pope Benedict XVI. *Compendium: Catechism of the Catholic Church*. U.S. Conference of Catholic Bishops, 2006.

Rhodes, Ron. *Reasoning from the Scriptures with Catholics*. Eugene: Harvest House, 2000.

Ryan, Kenneth. *Catholic Questions Catholic Answers*. Cincinnati: St. Anthony, 1990.

Sparagna. Aniceto M. *Personal Evangelism Among Roman Catholics: Practical and Doctrinal Suggestions of How to Win Catholics for Christ*. Joplin: College Press, 1935.

Schrotenboer, Paul G., ed. *Roman Catholicism: A Contemporary Evangelical Perspective*. Grand Rapids: Baker, 1988.

Tucker, Mancil. *Scriptural Names of the Lord's Church*. Pasadena: Haun, 1985.

Wilson, L.R. *Roman Catholicism: Facts or Fabrications*. Nashville: Voice of Freedom, 1965.

Webster's New World College Dictionary. 4th ed. 2001.

Zacchello, Joseph. *Ins and Outs of Romanism*. New York: Loizeaux, 1956.